# THE
# SNIPER

# THE SNIPER

## THE UNTOLD STORY OF
## THE MARINE CORPS' GREATEST
## MARKSMAN OF ALL TIME

## JIM LINDSAY

Foreword by
**Chuck Mawhinney**

ST. MARTIN'S PRESS
NEW YORK

First published in the United States by St. Martin's Press, an imprint of St. Martin's Publishing Group

THE SNIPER. Copyright © 2023 by Jim Lindsay. All rights reserved. Printed in the United States of America. For information, address St. Martin's Publishing Group, 120 Broadway, New York, NY 10271.

www.stmartins.com

Design by Meryl Sussman Levavi

Permission to reprint the map has been granted by Dan Guenther and Nick Zelinger of www.nzgraphics.com, originally published in the book *To the Sound of the Guns: 1st Battalion, 27th Marines from Hawaii to Vietnam 1966–1968* by Grady T. Birdsong, BirdQuill LLC, 2018.

Library of Congress Cataloging-in-Publication Data

Names: Lindsay, Jim, author. | Mawhinney, Chuck, 1949– writer of foreword.
Title: The sniper : the untold story of the Marine Corps' greatest marksman of all time / Jim Lindsay ; foreword by Chuck Mawhinney. Other titles: Untold story of the Marine Corps' greatest marksman of all time
Description: First edition. | New York : St. Martin's Press, 2023. | Identifiers: LCCN 2022048294 | ISBN 9781250282422 (hardcover) | ISBN 9781250282439 (ebook)
Subjects: LCSH: Mawhinney, Chuck, 1949– | United States. Marine Corps. Marine Regiment, 5th. Sniper Platoon— Biography. | Vietnam War, 1961–1975—Campaigns.
Classification: LCC DS558.4 .M3945 2023 | DDC 959.704/342092 [B]—dc23/eng/20221007
LC record available at https://lccn.loc.gov/2022048294

Our books may be purchased in bulk for promotional, educational, or business use. Please contact your local bookseller or the Macmillan Corporate and Premium Sales Department at 1-800-221-7945, extension 5442, or by email at MacmillanSpecialMarkets@macmillan.com.

First Edition: 2023

10   9   8   7   6   5   4   3   2   1

*For all the warriors who didn't come home*

# CONTENTS

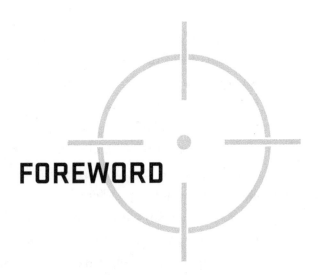

# FOREWORD

**M**y name is Charles Benjamin Mawhinney, known to most people as Chuck, unless you're family or someone I grew up with in Lakeview, Oregon, where I was always referred to as Charley. Our family on my dad's side seems to have three different names: Charles, William, and Benjamin. Lucky me, I got two of the three.

About thirty some years ago, after a long day of work on Friday night, there was a little tavern where all the working-class men would go called the Idle Hour. It was there that I met a man named Jim Lindsay, who was farming here in the valley. We struck up quite a few conversations and he invited me to go duck hunting on his place, as the river ran through his property. Well, with my love of hunting I had to go. All he really knew was I did like to hunt. We continued to see each other on occasion until one day someone mentioned at the tavern that Jim had sold his farm and moved back to the Willamette Valley. Damn Flatlander.

It had been a long time when Jim called me up and asked if he could stop by for a visit. I said, "Sure, come on over and we can talk old times." When he came in he brought a copy of this book called *The Little Bastards*. Seems like he did a lot of daydreaming about the era he had grown up in and took up writing a book about it. Since he had left he had apparently found out who I was, or at least what I had done in Vietnam, and I think it intrigued him. We talked awhile and I thanked him for coming by and giving me a copy of the book.

After reading the book I called him and told him I loved the book and it really reminded me of growing up during that time. We started talking a little more and he broached the subject of me ever having a book written about me. I told him I had worked with an author out of Florida for five years and just when the book was about done the guy had a heart attack and died. The book never got published. I told him I would never do another book. He would come over here every so often, as he still had some business in town, and drop by and bring up the book again. I finally agreed to a biography, but he had to promise me that he wouldn't change any of the stories I told him because I had read a few books written by and about people from the war in Vietnam, and having been there I guess you could say I call bullshit on some of the stuff. We also agreed it would be about my growing up with some of the antics I got into. I feel Jim has done an excellent job of the book and telling my story. I'm just a simple person and in Vietnam I was just doing my job.

—CHUCK MAWHINNEY

# AUTHOR'S NOTE

I knew Chuck Mawhinney before he was famous. We became friends while frequenting the same beer-drinking establishment—a sawmill tavern in Baker City, Oregon. He was a special person, a guy you're glad is in the room. Then I moved away and we lost touch.

Ten years later, I was surprised to see Chuck on TV and shocked to hear he'd been a marine sniper. He'd never mentioned it to me.

I researched him and was blown away by the many articles devoted to Chuck and his military achievements. I wanted to see him again and ask more about his life he'd hidden for so long. I wondered if he would remember me. Would he share his secrets with me? I wondered why no one had written a book about him.

I tracked him down through mutual friends. Over the phone, Chuck did remember me and invited me to his home. We met in his man-cave garage. Sitting on stools around a homemade table, we caught up over beers. He'd read and liked my first novel, *The Little Bastards.*

"I *was* one," he said with a smile.

I loved hearing that. "Would you mind talking about being a sniper?"

Chuck gave me a look—his total attention. Then, he slid his stool back and relaxed, smiling again. "What would you like to know, Jim?"

I sat on my stool, mesmerized, as he recounted his war experiences in his casual matter-of-fact way, often-times making fun of a life-threatening situation. He spoke of his colorful childhood in the mountain town of Lakeview, Oregon. Proudly, he talked of his family and his career in the US Forest Service.

What a life, I thought. The world needs to know this story.

"Chuck," I asked. "You've had such a life. Why hasn't anyone written a book about you?"

"One author tried and died during the process," Chuck said with a slight ironic smile.

Wow, I thought. Good thing I'm not superstitious.

"Chuck, I'd like to do it—write your story. You know, your biography."

He gave me that look again.

"It'd be fun!" I said. "And it's gonna take some beer."

He smiled and said, real serious-like, "Everything in the book has to be true—as true as I can remember it. And change my spotters' names. I was outed without my consent. I don't want to do that to anyone else."

We shook on it.

After that, we enjoyed hundreds of hours of interviews in his garage. In addition, I've researched the war in Vietnam, reading dozens of books and scouring the internet. But I wanted more. I wanted to feel the country Chuck described to me. I wanted to find his base, An Hoa: the heat, the smells, the snakes, and the bugs that had chewed on him.

I flew to Vietnam. I visited military bases and battle sites from Saigon to Hanoi. I visited with locals who told me of their love of Americans and their appreciation for what they'd tried to do for them. It was nice to hear that what Chuck and others did hasn't been forgotten.

I did find An Hoa, though it was overtaken by jungle. In horrific heat I walked the entire length of its abandoned airstrip, stepping over cow pies while slapping insects.

The Vietnam War was fought in my time. I'm proud of the soldiers who served. Some were my friends who didn't come back. I'm ashamed of the way our brave men were treated when they did come back.

I feel I owe them. I've worked hard to make Chuck's book the very best it can be.

As Chuck requested, everything in this book is true—as true as he can remember it. The spotters' names are changed, except for Sugar Bear, who is deceased. I've dramatized the events with dialogue and sensory details so readers can feel they're along for the ride.

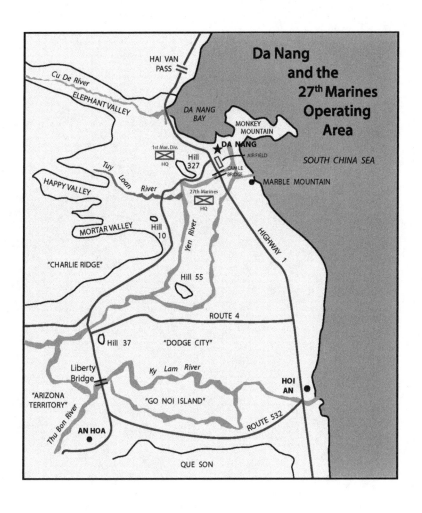

Da Nang
and the
27th Marines
Operating
Area

HAI VAN
PASS

Cu De River

ELEPHANT VALLEY

DA NANG
BAY

MONKEY
MOUNTAIN

DA NANG

AIR FIELD

SOUTH CHINA SEA

1st Mar. Div.

HQ

Hill
327

CAM LE
BRIDGE

MARBLE MOUNTAIN

Tuy

Loan

River

HAPPY VALLEY

27th Marines

HQ

MORTAR VALLEY

Hill
10

Yen River

"CHARLIE RIDGE"

Hill 55

HIGHWAY 1

ROUTE 4

Hill 37

"DODGE CITY"

Liberty
Bridge

Ky  Lam  River

HOI
AN

"ARIZONA
TERRITORY"

"GO NOI ISLAND"

Thu Bon River

AN HOA

ROUTE 532

QUE SON

# THE
# SNIPER

# PROLOGUE

**C**aptain Wiley turned to Chuck. "We've got a problem on our hands. I'd say half the NVA army is on its way to attack Da Nang. They need to be stopped or at least delayed."

"I know right where they'll cross the river," said Chuck. There was only one place where the river was shallow enough. Chuck had been a permanent fixture for more than a year and knew the Arizona Territory better than anyone. He was like the sheriff of the whole An Hoa Basin.

"If you go down to the river," said Wiley, "you'll get yourself killed."

"If I stay here," said Chuck, "we'll *all* get killed."

"Okay." Wiley sighed, shaking his head. "You see them and get back here on the double. Got it?"

"Got it, sir."

Chuck hurried to the men on the perimeter between him and the river and cleared the return signals and call signs. It was getting dark; he'd need the starlight scope. So he switched guns with his spotter Carter and they set out for the river, pushing through eight-foot-tall elephant grass on the way.

They arrived at the river where the grass was short and Chuck knew the murky water was shallow. Searching for a hide on the riverbank, they found a peninsula that offered cover and protection from enemy fire. It was perfect for a sitting-position rest for their rifles situated where they could see up and down the river where the NVA would cross.

Chuck set up his starlight scope. Through the green lens, even with the darkened sky of the monsoon rains, Chuck could make out trees on the opposite bank.

Soon he observed movement straight across from their position. A single soldier appeared, chest-deep in the water, his face green in the starlight scope. He wore an NVA pith helmet and held his rifle above his head.

Chuck figured he was a scout and hoped he wouldn't have to shoot him—it would be a catastrophe to kill the scout right in front of the enemy; they'd charge the river and find Delta 1/5 company and slaughter them.

Chuck steadied the reticle on him, mentally timing him as he crossed.

The scout came out of the river close to Chuck's position, climbed the bank, and stood still, close enough Chuck could hear water dripping off him. He turned and looked straight at Chuck as if seeing him. A chilling look. Chuck slipped off the safety. But the man looked away and moved past him toward the elephant grass. Chuck followed him with the reticle. He was not going to let the man get between him and the company. He held his breath and increased trigger pressure, ready to dispatch him.

The man turned around and reentered the river. Chuck breathed.

Carter whispered, "Do you think they're going to cross?"

"Yep," Chuck whispered back. "And there'll be a lot of 'em."

"What we gonna do?"

"We'll be here. And when they come, I'm gonna surprise 'em with a party. It's Valentine's Day, you know."

Chuck and Carter waited in the chilling rain for an hour. Then came the NVA soldiers, single file, wading into the river, holding their rifles high. Chuck's heart pounded as he trained the reticle on the center of the leader's forehead, staying on it as the men kept coming.

"Get ready to haul ass," Chuck whispered to Carter. "When I yell go, run for your life."

"I'm ready," Carter whispered.

Chuck squeezed off the first shot. Greenish blood blew out the back of the man's skull, sinking him, exposing the one behind him. Chuck sank that one. The column stopped and ducked low in the water, giving Chuck perfect green head-size targets. He fired rounds moving from head to head. Sixteen kills in less than thirty seconds. Pith helmets and bodies floated down the river.

# 1
# FIRST HIDE

**C**huck was sweltering, gun leveled through a hole in his hide. But even with the heat and the musty, dark conditions he was excited. *Keep calm*, he told himself. *Stay quiet and they will come.* He wondered from which way. He hoped he was downwind. Don't forget to smell and listen for them. Don't mind the spider crawling up your butt and let the fly alone—he needs a meal, too, you know.

Awhile later, the sun was straight-up hot, sweat running into his eyes, blurring his view of the path. *What's that scratching sound? Could it be them? No, just a rat. Hope it doesn't come in here, I'd have to let it gnaw my face off. And snakes—I've seen snakes here.*

His tongue was like sandpaper—he needed to drink but wouldn't let himself move. *Don't think of water or you might piss your pants.*

A small covey of quail appeared on the path, the big one the size of a football, topped with a plume that bobbed as he strutted along, pompous and important, continually calling the warning, "Chee-ca-go," as he herded the others who were jammed together, gawking nervous-like. Seeing no danger, the leader began to scratch and peck and they all joined in, eating the grain Chuck had baited them with.

Chuck trained his rifle sight on the leader and fingered the trigger. Squeeze, don't yank, he told himself. He got steady.

Between breaths he crushed the trigger—a giant explosion and flash tumbled Chuck over backward off the milk stool onto the floor of Grandpa's barn, his ears ringing. Flat on his back, his shoulder hurting terrible, Chuck cried.

The door on the outhouse slammed. "Chaulky, are you okay?" The barn door blew open with Grandpa's big frame filling the doorway.

Chuck squinted through tears at Grandpa's worried face. "I'm okay, I think." He moaned, trying to quit crying. "My shoulder hurts something awful."

Grandpa fell to his knees over Chuck. "You could've killed yourself. What were you thinking?"

"I wanted quail for supper. Just like when *you* shoot 'em."

"Next time ask me, okay, Chaulky?"

"Okay, Grandpa," he said, wiping his nose on the sleeve of his good arm.

Grandpa stood, picked up the smoking shotgun, opened the breech, then looked down at his four-year-old grandson. "No wonder it knocked you over. You pulled both triggers!" He leaned the gun against the wall. "Now, Chaulky, hold your arm close to your tummy and try not to move it. I'm going to pick you up gentle-like and take you to the hospital."

"Do we have to?"

"To fix your arm."

Chuck left the barn cradled in his Grandpa's arms and passed the quail strewn about.

"Wow, Grandpa, I got 'em all!"

It was a bumpy, painful ride in Grandpa's Chevy to the Lakeview hospital, where Chuck was diagnosed with a broken collarbone and equipped with a sling. His mom arrived shortly from the beauty parlor where she worked.

Grandpa took a good ass-chewing from Mom, who insisted that from then on, the shotgun would be kept unloaded and locked in Grandpa's closet.

Chuck learned by doing and, in this case, felt bad about the trouble he'd caused but also proud of putting food on the table. The next day's lunch was Chuck's quail.

# 2

# DOWN AT THE BAR
# WITH GRANDPA

**C**harles Benjamin Mawhinney was born on February 23, 1949, joining the family of father Charles Mawhinney, mother Beulah Mawhinney, three-year-old sister Veronica, and Beulah's father, William Franz, known to Chuck only as Grandpa.

They lived on Grandpa's farm in the tiny town of Pine Creek, Oregon, surrounded by pine-covered mountains. Grandpa's farm was small but nearly self-sufficient. He grew hay for the chickens, cows, and pigs. He butchered the pigs himself and cured the ham and bacon. He hunted wild game and canned it along with the vegetables from his garden and cherries from his orchard. Of course, the family helped him with all this—except for the hunting. Dad hadn't hunted since World War II. He'd been a marine and participated in the invasion of Guam and Guadalcanal, where he'd been shot up and sent home.

Pine Creek was nearly a mile high, making the winters cold and long, but, thanks to careful planning, they had plenty to eat, and the farmhouse was snug with woodstove warmth.

In the winter of 1953, Chuck was five years old, his collarbone healed. Dad worked at the sawmill, and Mom styled hair in the nearby town of Lakeview, where Veronica went to second grade. So, except for weekends, Chuck spent most of his time with Grandpa.

Chuck liked the barn and rolled out early with Grandpa to see if there had been a baby born in the night or several, like a new litter of pigs. (Chuck never needed sex education; he caught the drift of it early on.) It was warm and noisy in the barn with the heat from the animals and all the clucking and squealing. The critters were glad to see Chuck in the morning. He petted them and was good for a little extra hay or grain, and they knew it.

On snowstormy mornings, the family would eat a hot breakfast, then Mom and Dad would dig the car out, load up Veronica, and follow the snowplow, slipping and sliding on the ice and snow toward Lakeview.

Enjoying the heat off the woodstove, and close

enough to the radio to hear Jack Benny and *The Lone Ranger*, Chuck and Grandpa listened the winter days away. Chuck pushed his little car over the wooden floor until the wheels fell off. He needed new toys, like the Lone Ranger cap pistol and BB gun in the Montgomery Ward catalog. He knew that catalog like the pope knew the Bible.

One evening after dinner, Mom was at the kitchen table folding clothes. Chuck saw his chance. He slid the open catalog onto the table in front of her and said, "Can I have one of these?" pointing to the Lone Ranger cap pistol.

"Those things cost money, Charley," Mom said.

"How can I get money?"

"Work for it," she said.

"How? I'm too young to get a job."

"These things will come in time," Mom assured him.

Chuck felt stuck. He needed that pistol but he had no way of earning the money for it.

After an eternity, the snow began to melt.

"Hey, Chaulky." Grandpa was talking from his side of the kitchen table with a mouthful of roast beef sandwich. They were having lunch; Grandpa was pretty handy at making something out of last night's meal.

"How about us walk into town after eating? What do you think?"

"Good idea, Grandpa. What we gonna do in town?"

"Maybe we'll get some candy."

"That's a real good idea, Grandpa." Chuck had been to town before with Mom and Dad, but this was going to be a first with just him and Grandpa. Pretty good stuff, Chuck was thinking.

"We gotta dress warm," said Grandpa. "It's still cold out there, you know."

Chuck hurried to his room, peeled off his pants, pulled on his long underwear, tugged on his jeans, dressed in a flannel shirt, and wrapped himself in his warm wool coat. Then he sock-footed it to the woodstove and pulled on his red-banded black rubber boots he'd warmed by the fire.

Restless, he got out first, waiting in the sun for Grandpa, marveling at the snow-covered mountains sparkling under blue sky.

After suffering the long winter, spring was a big deal for Chuck. He took in the fresh smell of the first spring thaw he could remember. Being only five, he could hardly remember last summer. It had flitted away so fast—turning to fall and freezing the tomatoes.

Now there was color all around him. Poking up through the melting snow was even some grass he hadn't seen for months, and the willow tree had buds on it. The sun warmed his back as he listened to ice melting off the eaves of the house, and birds ragging and flirting. A whole new world had opened up.

It was nice to be outside.

Grandpa came out pulling on his coat and quickly shut the door behind him to save the heat in the house—a heavy door that had never seen a key. He sucked in the cold fresh air. "Damn, Chaulky, it's good to be alive."

Together they stepped through the slush of the spring thaw.

"Careful, Chaulky," Grandpa said. "Driveway's slippery."

"Okay, Grandpa." *Plop!* Chuck went down hard on his behind. "Owee!" he cried, getting up rubbing his bottom.

"Told you so."

On the street stood giant icebergs left behind by the snowplows. Spring had made the street busy with traffic. No sidewalks, so Grandpa walked carefully between puddles and rivers with Chuck following close, ready to dodge cars and log trucks trying to drown him in spraying water. Chuck thought it all a great adventure, stomping and splashing his way through the deepest torrents. He waved at people shoveling snow, digging out. They smiled back. Chuck felt happiness in the air.

After a few blocks they were in the center of town, where the streets were completely plowed, cars moving about and log trucks fueling up at the gas station.

Downtown was small, but to Chuck it had big buildings, like Butler's market and a church. Facing Main Street was a row of buildings with a long, covered boardwalk like in the western movies fronted with a wooden rail to tie up horses. But no horses today.

Grandpa and Chuck stepped onto the boardwalk and stomped the snow off their boots. Chuck liked the boardwalk—Grandpa walking on it sounded just like on *The Lone Ranger, clop, clop, clop.* A lady walked toward them, careful-like, maybe worrying her high heels would get caught in the cracks between the boards.

"Howdy, ma'am," Grandpa said.

"How are you gents today?" Smiling, she passed by.

The first storefront they came to had a darkened window filled with electric signs. Chuck couldn't read yet so didn't know what they said. They walked past a bench, and Grandpa stopped at a shop door, but before he grabbed the knob, the door opened, jingling a bell. A man stepped out, pocketing some change. The bell jingled again as the door closed behind him. He dropped a dime and before he could nab it, it disappeared into a crack between the boards in the boardwalk.

"Damn," the guy said to Grandpa, laughing at himself. "There goes another one. Bet there's a fortune down there," and walked off.

"No fooling," Grandpa called after him. "Sorry about that."

*Oh boy,* Chuck thought, remembering the dime

flashing in the sun before it disappeared down the crack. Chuck's mind raced to the Montgomery Ward catalog and back to the dime under the boardwalk, wondering how he could get his hands on that fortune down there.

Grandpa opened the shop door, tripping the bell that reverberated through the tiny general store.

"Well hi!" said the lady clerk behind the cash register by the door. "Who's this little fella?"

"This here's my grandson, Chaulky. Chaulky, this is Flo. Flo, I need to see the boys for just a minute, would you mind showing Chaulky the candy rack?"

Chuck's ears perked up.

"Sure!" She winked at Grandpa. "I need another man in my life."

"Chaulky," said Grandpa, "take these two nickels and see if you can get a deal on some candy."

"Okay, Grandpa!" Chuck jingled the coins in his hand, slobbering and thinking of candy.

Grandpa disappeared into the darkness of the side door. The lady showed Chuck all the different candies in the rack of many-colored wrappers, and explained what each tasted like: Hot Tamales, Charms candy sour balls, Baby Ruth chocolate bars, Dubble Bubble chewing gum, Lucky Strike candy cigarettes . . .

With a good mouthful of sour balls going, Chuck was studying the candy rack for next time, when Grandpa appeared. He put his big hand on Chuck's shoulder,

his face serious looking, and cleared his throat, like
this was going to be important. "You're coming with
me into the next room. It's different than other stores
you've been. But as far as your mom is concerned, we
went to town to the *store*. You got it, Chaulky? Can you
keep mum?"

"Okay, Grandpa." Chuck didn't understand but
trusted Grandpa.

"Hey, Flo, can you bring me an Oly and Chaulky a
Roy Rogers?"

Ready for adventure and pumped with sugar, Chuck
followed Grandpa into the darkness. He smelled smoke
from cigars and the woodstove in the middle of the
room—Grandpa's aroma whenever he came home from
town. Chuck followed him past a bar that smelled of
stale beer, Grandpa walking sure, like in his pasture;
Chuck, not so much. It was dark and spooky in there
and high up on the walls were big animal heads with
horns, staring at Chuck with eyes that never left him.
He clamped onto Grandpa's pant leg.

"Chaulky, I want you to meet some friends of mine."

From around Grandpa's leg Chuck saw scary men
sitting around the stove. They had beards and were old
and grungy looking.

"This is my grandson, Chaulky."

Laid back in worn overstuffed chairs, they gave
Chuck a blank look. Stern looking. But Grandpa knew

them, so Chuck figured they must be okay. But he still feared them.

One grinned at him. "You takin' care of the old fart today?" he asked, thumbing toward Grandpa.

"Don't pay attention to these old fossils, Chaulky," Grandpa said.

From behind the bar, Flo set up their drinks. Grandpa lifted Chuck onto a barstool, sat on the stool next to him, and swiveled to face his friends. Chuck rode the stool from where he could see the rows of fancy bottles behind the bar, and began to spin, catching sight of himself in the mirror as he whirled past until he got dizzy and decided to stop and sip his drink for a while.

As the frozen firewood hissed next to the stove that popped and snapped, Chuck had a front-row seat, watching and listening as the old men sitting in chairs that didn't match spilled out stories Chuck only half understood. When Chuck and Grandpa finished their Roy Rogers and Oly, Grandpa said so long to the boys and Flo, and Chuck waved goodbye. The door jingled as they stepped out, and Grandpa said, "Chaulky, don't believe everything you hear around the stove."

"Okay, Grandpa." Though confused, Chuck figured that in time, he'd know what he meant.

Following Grandpa past the bench, he noticed a knothole in the boardwalk, remembered the lost dime and the man saying *bet there's a fortune down there.* That knothole was access to it.

Chuck kept Grandpa's secret. Each time they went to town Chuck tried a different brand of candy and, while Grandpa talked to his friends around the woodstove, he'd sip his Roy Rogers, thinking about when he'd get a chance at that fortune.

One sunny afternoon in May, they entered the store and were met by loud music and cussing through the door of the bar along with Flo's laughter.

Chuck couldn't wait to go in but Grandpa stopped and said, "Chaulky, I don't think you should go in there today. Flo will be back real soon and you can buy some candy." He handed him a dime. "And it's a nice day. Maybe go outside and look around—not too far though, okay?"

"Okay, Grandpa!" Chuck pocketed the dime and hurried out to the boardwalk.

When the coast was clear he dropped to his knees and peered through the knothole into the darkness. He saw bars of sunshine beaming on the dirt but no coins. Disappointed but determined, he discovered that by moving just so, and getting his nose right down where the air was musty, then lining up the light just right— yowie! The coins sparkled and winked back at him like in a pirate's chest.

Grandpa had taught him to keep a secret. Chuck had his own now. By keeping mum, he'd have the whole pile for himself. Soon he'd be a pistol-toting cowboy. But how to get the treasure?

From trying the different candies, he'd learned Dubble Bubble was sticky, which gave him an idea. Back at home, he cut a willow switch. Jawing the gum, he pulled a nickel from his pocket and dropped it at his feet. He stuck the wet and rubbery gum on the end of the stick, poked the nickel, carefully lifted it, peeled it off, put it in his pocket, and smiled to himself.

The next time at the store with Grandpa, he was ready, his stick under his coat.

"Hi Flo," said Grandpa, handing Chuck a dime.

"Hey Chaulky," said Flo. "Ya wanna Roy Rogers?"

"No ma'am. I think I'll just have a Dubble Bubble and play outside."

"Good idea, Chaulky," she said. "Get some sunshine."

Chuck bought some Dubble Bubbles with his Grandpa's money and stepped out, jingling the bell and jawing the gum. Sitting on the bench, he looked both ways and, seeing the coast was clear, he baited the willow switch, dropped to his knees, lowered the gum end of the switch through the knothole until it hit bottom, and pulled it up. All he got was dirty gum. He plucked it off the switch and worked the gum with his fingers to get it sticky again. The bell jingled and he jumped on the bench.

"What's you doing, honey?" a smiling lady said.

"Nothing, ma'am." Chuck palmed the gum.

The lady disappeared around the corner.

Just when Chuck was back to mining, a pickup truck pulled up and he leapt on the bench again.

Stepping onto the boardwalk, the truck driver said, "Whatcha doing, kid?"

"Nothin'," said Chuck, thinking, *If you'd leave me alone I could get back to my treasure.*

After several more failed attempts, getting dirt and getting interrupted, he pulled up a dime. He wanted to shout from the rooftops and run up and down the street like a drunken miner but he kept his cool and pocketed the coin. Just when he was going for more, the bell jingled. He stood up and there was Grandpa.

"Let's go, Chaulky."

Reluctantly, he replied, "Okay, Grandpa." He gave the knothole a hungry look, promising it he would be back.

By the time Chuck was six years old, he wasn't rich, but he had his Lone Ranger pistol and a few coins to jingle in his pocket. It was only a few dollars, but he made it himself and it was a good lesson about what a little hard work and ingenuity can get you.

During that year of going to town and sitting by the bar's woodstove with Grandpa, Chuck figured out the old men in time. He learned what they had done for a living by the way they still dressed. The loggers wore leather boots and work pants axed off above the ankle and held up by suspenders over striped shirts. A painter wore overalls with paint still on them. And then there was a rancher: tall and proud, wearing his big hat and boots.

And with Grandpa's help he learned how to decipher the truth from the fiction that flowed around the woodstove.

Later in school, Chuck would learn these men had won World War I just to return home to the 1918 Spanish flu pandemic, then just eleven years later plunged into the Great Depression while rearing the children who would win World War II.

# 3

# SHOOTING GRANDPA

In late spring of his sixth year, Chuck noticed Grandpa
pacing in his cherry orchard and waving his big arms, trying to cuss the blackbirds away, except they weren't listening. Grandpa was proud of his little cherry orchard
and kept it up, summer, fall, and winter, manicuring
and spraying and doting over it. Now the cherries had
begun to turn red, and the birds were stealing them.

Chuck wished he could help somehow. He picked up
a pebble off the driveway and joined Grandpa in the orchard. Chuck hurled the pebble at the nearest bird and
missed. Unimpressed, the bird flew to the next tree.

"Sorry, Grandpa."

"Thanks, Chaulky," Grandpa said. "We need to find a way to run them off, and soon."

The next morning was Saturday. Chuck followed the fragrance of bacon into the kitchen where Mom was cooking breakfast. Seeing Grandpa was missing, he sat down with Dad at the kitchen table.

"Where's Grandpa?" Chuck asked Dad.

"He left early for Lakeview—didn't say why."

"You hungry, Charley?" asked Mom.

"Oh boy, yea," said Chuck.

Later that morning, collecting eggs in the barn, Chuck heard Grandpa's Chevy pull into the driveway. Chuck blew out of the barn door and ran down the drive with an egg in each hand. Grandpa was standing by his car door holding a little rifle. Chuck hadn't seen a gun since his quail-shooting episode. The little rifle shone in Grandpa's big hands. It looked just like the Lone Ranger's Winchester but Chuck's size. It was the same one Chuck had drooled over in the Sears catalog: a Daisy Red Ryder.

"Wow, Grandpa!"

"Soon as you can shoot it, you're goin' after them blackbirds. Okay?"

"Okay, Grandpa!" he said, thinking how the Lone Ranger would do it.

"Here, hold this." Grandpa offered the gun to Chuck.

Chuck set the eggs gently on the ground and took

the little rifle in his hands. It was weighty and real feeling. The wooden stock was warm but the metal barrel was cool and smelled of oil. With the stock tucked into his shoulder Chuck pointed at a fence post and sighted down the barrel.

"Don't step on the eggs," said Grandpa.

Confused, Chuck swung back around.

"And keep the barrel down! Don't point it at anyone you don't want to shoot."

Chuck instantly tipped the barrel down and stepped away from the eggs.

"Come with me—we need to make a target." Grandpa tromped off toward the barn. Chuck, barrel down, followed him into the darkness, hearing pigs snorting. Grandpa went straight to the workbench, reached up to a shelf, brought down a shoebox, and pulled off the lid. "This oughta do it." He picked up a hammer and a couple of nails. "We'll need these, too."

They left and closed the door behind them. Grandpa nailed the shoebox lid to the door sideways at Chuck's eye level. He pulled a carpenter's pencil from his bib's chest pocket, drew three circles about the size of water glasses, and colored them in.

Chuck hurried along behind Grandpa as he paced his way back toward the car, ". . . seven, eight, nine." Looking back at the barn, Grandpa said, "This is about right, I'd guess."

The targets looked pretty small to Chuck.

"Okay, Chaulky. Let's load her up." Grandpa pulled a small clear plastic bag from his bib's pants pocket and tore a corner off it with his teeth. "Trade ya."

Chuck handed him the gun. Grandpa handed over the bag. Holding the heavy little bag in his hand, Chuck could see the little round golden BBs and feel them roll between his fingers.

Holding the gun, Grandpa pulled the shot-tube magazine out from under the barrel, took the bag, and dribbled the BBs into the magazine one by one. "Now then, here's how to cock it." Holding the gun by its forearm, he pulled up on the lever until it clicked. "Now it's loaded."

He handed the gun back to Chuck, barrel down. "Aim at the target, just like you did the quail."

Chuck put the bead on the target, worrying that it was going to hurt like before.

"Steady now, hold your breath and squeeze the trigger."

*POP! Thud.* Chuck lowered the barrel and squinted at the target, looking for a hole.

"You missed the circle," Grandpa said.

*Darn!* At least it hadn't hurt his shoulder.

"But you hit the lid," said Grandpa. "See the dot in the lower left corner?"

Chuck was happy then. And ready to do it again.

His shooting career had begun.

"Okay, Chaulky, cock it like I showed you."

Chuck pulled up on the lever with all his might but couldn't pull it far enough to make it click. So, he pointed the gun straight down, rested the muzzle on a rock, and with both hands pushed the lever down until it clicked.

He shot at the target. *POP!* But no thud. He looked at Grandpa, bewildered. "I missed the whole barn!"

"You didn't have a BB in the chamber. Since you're cocking it upside down, you'll have to load the BBs directly into the barrel." Grandpa took the gun and unloaded the BBs. "Put these in your pocket."

Chuck dropped a BB into the end of the barrel, shot, and hit the box lid closer to a circle. After a dozen or so shots, he began drilling the targets. They looked like they had the measles.

"Okay, Chaulky, you can hit the target good and cock and reload, so go after 'em." He pointed to the flock feasting on his cherries, turned on his heel, and hurried off to the outhouse.

Elated to begin the hunt, keeping the barrel raised so the BB wouldn't roll out, Chuck crept to the orchard. High in the branches above him, the birds were busy robbing cherries. Close then, he took aim at a fat one, held his breath, squeezed the trigger, and *POP!* they flew away. None fell. He'd missed. Darn.

Determined, Chuck stalked the blackbirds relentlessly that day. Hour after hour, he blazed away, missing every shot, but at least he scared them off for a bit.

The next day he got a feather. The day after that, one of the birds pitched off a limb, fell at his feet, and flopped around open-mouthed, its little chest heaving.

"I got 'im!"

It quit breathing and got still. Chuck stared down at the bird, shiny black feathers, toes like his chickens' sticking up. Not a pretty bird—especially now that it had been shot. Chuck picked it up. It was almost weightless. Its tummy was fuzzy and soft and still warm.

The bird looked back at him with accusing eyes. *Why did you kill me?*

Chuck suddenly felt like a murderer, but whispered, "Because you stole Grandpa's cherries."

A new flock flashed over low, warbling, preparing to land in the orchard. The commotion wiped out Chuck's pang of guilt. He dropped the dead bird to show to Grandpa later. He had a job to do.

After that, the flocks lost more and more flyers. Chuck began head-shooting them, then eye-shooting them. Between flocks he shot flies off the barn wall and that spring saved most of the cherries—Grandpa's little hero.

Until one day, Grandpa was high up on a ladder picking cherries when a whole squadron of birds circled overhead. Chuck decided to flock shoot 'em to see if he could hit one on the fly.

*POP!* "*Ouch!*" Grandpa yelled. The birds braked and fluttered off in all directions. Grandpa stomped down the ladder holding a bucket of cherries in one hand and the side of his behind with the other.

*Uh-oh.* Chuck held out the gun, flat on his palms, knowing Grandpa was going to take it away.

"I don't want that damn thing," Grandpa steamed. "I just want you to know where in hell you're shooting at. You got that?"

"Yes, Grandpa." He would never forget that lesson.

Late that summer, Chuck moved with Dad, Mom, and Veronica into an old two-story house in Lakeview where Chuck would be starting school. It was a quiet neighborhood with paved streets and real cement sidewalks.

But Grandpa stayed on the farm. Chuck didn't understand why Grandpa didn't come along, too. He was sad he wouldn't see Grandpa every day and help with his chores. He missed the pigs and chickens, too.

A few days later at lunchtime, he and Mom were meeting over grilled cheese sandwiches and tomato soup. Mom was teary-eyed.

"What's wrong, Mom?"

"I don't know how to tell you, Charley. Your grandfather died."

"Well," said Chuck. "Someone better tell Grandpa then."

At supper, Dad tried. "Charley, your grandpa died, and we're going to have a funeral."

"I miss Grandpa—we should go visit him."

Chuck just couldn't connect the dots.

Chuck fidgeted on the iron-hard pew, between Veronica and his mom, who was sobbing again. She'd been crying a lot lately, which worried Chuck. Dad's arm was wrapped around Mom and occasionally he dangled his fingers in Chuck's hair. The only thing wrong was that Grandpa hadn't showed up yet and they hadn't saved a seat for him.

Directly in front of Chuck was a huge shiny wooden box with handles, covered with flowers. Chuck liked the flowers' colors and shapes but not the smell they put off. They reeked. Behind the box stood a solemn-looking man dressed in a dark suit and tie.

Organ music started. The man swayed with the music, looking down at the box, then raised sad eyes and looked over the crowd.

Chuck twisted in the pew and looked back. "Where's Grandpa?"

Veronica rolled her eyes at him like he was saying a bad joke. Chuck was confused. Grandpa was part of the family. "He should be here. I think the funeral has started."

The music stopped. The solemn man cleared his throat. "Let us pray."

It got quiet. Everyone dropped their chins, so Chuck did, too. He looked at his shoes, worrying about Grandpa.

"Here lies William Franz!" the solemn man shouted.

Chuck jumped. Who was William Franz? The solemn man continued talking real nice about this man Franz.

The music started again, then the crowd prayed again and then it got real still. Chuck fidgeted—Grandpa still hadn't shown up. The solemn man motioned to the usher, then looked up at the ceiling, flinging his arms into the air, and the usher threw the lid open on the box. The crowd gasped.

*What's happening?* wondered Chuck.

Then he saw Grandpa in the box, suited up and resting on a fancy pillow.

Chuck jumped up, waving his hands. "Get up, Grandpa! We're having a funeral!"

Grandpa didn't answer. Chuck ran to his side. Grandpa was gray and still. Not breathing. Like the blackbird. Chuck finally realized Grandpa was dead. He would never see his real grandpa again. Chuck held back and didn't cry—the Lone Ranger didn't cry.

That night, he cried himself to sleep.

# 4

# ALMOST KILLING
# LARRY STEEN

Late in the summer following his first year in school, seven-year-old Chuck noticed a family unloading furniture across the street. Not to be nosy, but curious as heck, he spied from behind a bush in his side yard. He perked up when a kid about his age came out of the house wearing a cowboy hat and carrying a BB gun and sat on the front steps. Chuck ran into the house. "Hey, Mom!"

"Shut the screen door behind you before every fly in the neighborhood comes in." Mom dried her hands on her apron.

Chuck pulled it shut. "The new neighbor kid has a BB gun."

"Well, go introduce yourself, but be careful with your guns, okay?"

"Sure, Mom."

Chuck ran to his room, got his gun, pulled on his cowboy hat, and hurried across the street. The boy looked up. Chuck stopped on the sidewalk. "Hey, my name's Charley. What's yours?"

"Dennis. We're moving in. I'm gonna start second grade here."

"So am I. I see you got a gun. Can you hit anything with it?"

"Yea, mostly birds and such. I've shot cats. They don't like it a lot. What about you?"

"I shot my Grandpa once. He didn't like it much, either. You ever shoot flies off a wall?"

"You can do that?"

"Yeah, come on. I'll show ya."

And a lifelong friendship was born.

Nothing was safe when the boys were on the prowl with their BB guns. Like their neighbor's tulips. They were her pride and joy. To Chuck and Dennis they were simply multicolored targets that would shatter on impact.

She'd yell at them, "Stop shooting my flowers, or I'll call the police!"

And the boys would hang their heads in mock remorse. "We're sorry, Miss Osgood!"

She'd blush. "Well, just don't do it again."

Then they'd shoot 'em up the next day.

Most of the boys in the neighborhood had BB guns, and Chuck was ready for bigger targets. The inevitable happened: BB gun wars. Backyard battles.

That fall, during a chilly nighttime engagement, Chuck and Dennis, noses running from the cold, crept through backyards carrying their trusty BB guns.

Chuck detected movement in a tree above. An enemy combatant was hunkered down on a low branch, pointing a slingshot right at Chuck. Reacting in a flash, Chuck shot from the hip, *POP! Thud*—hitting the enemy dead center in the chest. He flipped forward off the limb, just like on TV, landing on his back right in front of Chuck.

It was Larry Steen with his Wham-O slingshot next to him, marble still in it.

"What's wrong with him?" Dennis asked. "He's not breathing."

"*Damn!*" said Chuck, horrified, "I think I *killed* him."

The other boys gathered around and leaned over Larry, snot dripping on the body.

"His mom ain't gonna like this," someone said.

Larry snorted and began to breathe. So did Chuck.

Landing on the hard ground had merely knocked the wind out of Larry.

After that near disaster, the boys evolved from BB gun wars. And, miraculously, could still wink with either eye.

# 5

# HUNTING FROM
# THE SKY

In the spring of Chuck's fourteenth year, his dad and two friends went in together on an airplane and began flying out of the Lakeview airport. It was an old bird, a Taylorcraft, slow and fragile. But it was an airplane, with wheels and a motor and a throttle, and it was fun. So of course Chuck got his nose right in it, helping the three partners upgrade the engine and shorten the wings, which gave the old girl more speed and maneuverability.

Chuck wanted to take flying lessons, but that cost money. He needed a summer job.

Lakeview had a Ford dealership. It was a proud concern where suits and ties were worn and a handshake meant something. The owner, Jim Farley, was a pleasant man who knew everyone for hundreds of miles. He had a great clientele and a steady workforce. People spent their entire careers working at Farley Ford. Somehow Chuck Mawhinney, at fourteen years old, wrangled a job out of Jim Farley.

Chuck started as the wash boy. He washed half the cars one day and the other half the next. After proudly cashing his first payroll check, he started flying lessons.

When school started, Chuck kept working at Farley Ford on Saturdays. When winter came and the hose froze up, Farley moved him into the garage, detailing used cars.

It was a great stroke of luck for Chuck to land a job inside the garage. He liked the cars and the smell of gas and oil and new tires. It was exciting for him when the new cars rolled off the trucks out front in the street. After his fifteenth birthday he got to drive them into the garage, where he polished them for the showroom.

Early the following summer, Chuck got his aircraft solo license and flew all over. But it wasn't fun flying alone. So, he decided to take Dennis. They'd beg a ride to the airport. Dennis would hide in the sagebrush at the end of the runway. Chuck would taxi down, turn around, and fiddle with the wing flaps while Dennis hopped in. Then they'd fly off.

Late that summer, word came that the ranches were getting eaten up by jackrabbits, so the ranchers were welcoming any help they could get. The boys began taking their .22 rifles. From the sky, they searched the hayfields until they saw the rabbits. Chuck would swoop down, level out over the haystacks, then he and Dennis would blaze away out of both doors, roll out, and come back, *ack ack ack*.

Deer season was approaching, so Charley and Dennis took the plane to scout deer for a motorcycle hunt during the season.

After searching the sagebrush with no luck, Chuck decided on Crane Mountain, known for monster bucks. He peeled off, crossed the valley, and entered Crane Canyon. Searching the pine-covered slopes for deer, Chuck flew slow, looking down out of the left window with Dennis sitting behind, scanning out the right side.

The canyon got steeper and narrower. Suddenly Chuck glanced ahead and saw the side of Crane Mountain looming. He ran out of canyon and airspeed and ideas all at the same time. The plane stalled and they fell. Chuck did the only thing he could have done to save their lives; he kicked the left rudder to fall nose down. The motor strained, the treetops coming closer. Just as the plane started clipping pine needles, it picked up enough airspeed to stay off the trees all the way down the mountain.

As soon as Chuck stopped the plane at the hangar,

Dennis leapt out. Chuck climbed out, really impressed with himself, and spied a small pine branch caught in a wheel. Grinning after Dennis, who was headed for the highway, Chuck yelled, "I told you I was good!"

# 6
# HERO

**A**round Christmastime, when he was still fifteen, Chuck acquired an old '50 Chevy coupe and counted off the days until February 23, his sixteenth birthday, when he could drive it legally.

On February 23, he was the first customer at the DMV. A mechanic at the dealership had shuffled his car to the DMV for him. "Don't make me come back and get you," teased the mechanic, putting even more pressure on Chuck to pass the test.

He walked out like he'd grown a foot, his freshly minted license in his billfold, and drove away in his own car.

Now that he had his driver's license, Mr. Farley let him take new cars on test-drives. Mustang fastbacks and Galaxies with big motors and four-speeds needed a lot of test-driving, and Chuck was there, handy on the job to take care of it. He liked to burn rubber, and he had a whole fleet of new cars with those little new tires at his command.

In addition, the mechanics often asked him to test used cars. One day, a mechanic tossed him some car keys and said, "Hey, Charley, take this old Merc out and see if I got that rattle fixed under the dash."

"Sure, Dean!" Chuck pulled out of the garage in a 1957 Mercury and drove for Smith Loop, known for its potholes. He couldn't make the Merc rattle, so he U-turned and whizzed back on the highway.

Entering Lakeview, he slowed for traffic. Poking along in front of him was a guy on a motorcycle with a little girl riding on the back. Chuck pulled on his blinker to go by. As he was passing, the guy, without signaling or looking back, turned left for his driveway. Chuck saw terror in the little girl's eyes. All he could do to save her was drive around them. He hit the gas, yanked the wheel, and ran into the ditch, skidding until the Merc hit a massive tree.

He woke up with his head rammed into the steering wheel, the windshield coated in blood, and most of his upper teeth all over the dashboard.

Charley saved the little girl's life that day, and has lived his life without his own front teeth as a reminder.

# 7

# BUSTED FOR MIP

**C**huck and Dennis had started experimenting with alcohol in their early teens, when a neighbor kid shared his parents' liquor cabinet with them. The next morning Chuck awoke in his family's camp trailer with a yellow MIP (a ticket for a minor found in possession of alcohol) pinned to his shirt. Someone had called the police, who'd found Chuck unconscious on the floor.

Being a workingman, Chuck carried cash in his wallet and usually a pack of cigarettes in his pocket. He began hanging around with older kids who had connections. He went to beer busts in a gravel pit outside town and partied up at Drews Reservoir. When he got his license to drive, the car became a rolling liquor store. Chuck was popular and fun, but he wasn't too shrewd or careful with his drinking, so he got caught drinking often.

By the time Chuck turned seventeen he'd racked up a bunch of MIPs. Because he had a job, he could pay the bail and never had to go to court. But getting caught by the cops was embarrassing—especially to his city cop dad.

The start of the first semester of his senior year, Chuck enrolled in a school-to-work program with Farley Ford, which meant more hours, which meant more money. With this windfall, Chuck became financially independent and could merely pay off his MIPs out of his own pocket and continue his wild-ass life.

Mom tried to talk to Chuck about it. She'd take in a deep breath and then, letting out a sigh, would say with sad eyes, "Charley, what's to become of you?"

Chuck would say, "I'll be okay, Mom."

Meanwhile, unknown to Chuck, a perfect parental "good cop/bad cop" scenario had developed, with his dad being the literal bad cop. He was talking with John Vandenberg, the Lakeview juvenile officer, about Chuck's record. "What in the hell am I going to do about my boy Charley? Nothing his mother and I have tried seems to get to him. We need some help."

"Yeah, I agree," John said. "If we don't get a handle on him we'll need another file cabinet. Charley's about got this one filled up."

"Do you think a little jail time would open his eyes?"

"Wouldn't hurt to try," said John. "Maybe a weekend would do it. But first we'll have to catch him with some beer again so we'll have something to arrest him for."

"We won't have long to wait, I'm afraid. He's always got beer in his car."

Saturday night, Chuck made a beer run to Chiloquin, ninety miles northwest of Lakeview on the Klamath Indian Reservation. With its own traditions and laws, it was like another country. Grocery stores sold beer to anyone, so Chuck and his friends would periodically get a few cases and stash them in woodpiles around town.

Returning to Lakeview after dark, Chuck passed a black-and-white hiding behind the "Welcome to Lakeview" sign and flinched. *Damn.*

The cop spun around and flipped on his red light.

Hitting the brakes, Chuck wondered, *How'd he know I was coming into town?*

Both hands on the wheel, looking straight ahead, he heard the crunch of boots in the gravel.

"Where you been tonight, Charley?"

"Just went for a ride, sir."

"Give me your keys. I wanna see what you got in your trunk."

"There's nothing in there, sir, really."

"Give 'em up."

The next Friday after school, the cell door clanged shut behind him, ringing in his ears as he stared in horror at the steel toilet hanging on the wall next to a steel sink, beside a steel bunk bed with army blankets covering a bare mattress and no pillow.

When the officer had arrested Chuck on Saturday night, he'd made him transfer the beer into his trunk and followed Chuck down to city hall, where he was given a written reservation for a weekend in jail, starting the next Friday. He drove home late. Dad sat quietly while Chuck told his mom, which was hard for Chuck and his mom. The next day at work he told Jim Farley, and old Farley didn't like it much. Then somehow the word got out, and Dennis and everyone at school thought it was funnier than shit. When Friday finally arrived, Chuck was relieved to start his sentence. Homework in hand, he had showed up for jail at 5 p.m.

High above the top bunk was a barred window. Seeing daylight, Chuck climbed the bunk, reached through the bars, opened the window, and looked three stories down to the alley full of garbage cans and other human debris. There was no busting out. He threw himself onto the lower bunk's lumpy mattress and began his homework. He finished it shortly and then: nothing. Time stopped. He stared out the cell door at the lonely hallway, thinking of his friends on the outside hustling girls while he listened to alley cats yowl.

Saturday was a long, long day of hating the cop who'd arrested him and the jailer who banged on the bars to feed him shit called food. Chuck took stock of his life, thinking, *I better leave Lakeview before I get into a whole lot* more *trouble.* He plotted how. *I like to fly. After graduation I might just join the Navy or the Air Force.* The thought of soaring through the skies with machine guns at his fingertips, carrying a load of bombs—and the machismo that came with that— appealed to him. *I've already shot game out of a plane, so doing it for the military shouldn't be too hard.*

Saturday night came, and Chuck could hear a band playing rock'n'roll in the Memorial Hall just across the alley from his cell. If not for the bars in his window, Chuck could almost leap that far.

Later that night, between sets, he heard hollering from down in the alley.

Chuck crawled up on the top bunk and looked out. It was Dennis and some of the other guys. Dennis was grinning up at him, plastered, stumbling around with a bottle in his fist. "Hey, Charley," he slurred. "The band's really hot. So're the girls. The hall's full of 'em. Why don't you come down and drink some beer with us?"

*If I could break outta here,* Chuck thought, *and the jump didn't kill me, I'd strangle every son of a bitchin' one of 'em.* He rolled over and wadded himself in the army blanket, hoping to block out all the fun he was missing.

When Chuck got out Sunday evening he walked straight to Dennis's house to deliver some revenge for making fun of him while he was jailed up.

Dennis's mom opened the door.

"Where's Dennis?" Chuck asked.

Worried-looking, she said, "That's what we'd like to know. He didn't come home from the dance and hasn't called."

"Really?" It wasn't like Dennis to go off without him. Hoping Dennis wasn't hurt somewhere, Chuck pretended for her sake not to be worried. "He'll show up. He probably fell in love and followed some girl home. I heard there were a lot of girls at the dance. He'll be home tonight—he's gotta go to school tomorrow."

"I hope so." She quietly closed the door.

*I wish I knew where to look*, thought Chuck, *but he's always been with me. Wish the little son of a bitch would call.*

Chuck's phone didn't ring. It was a long night.

Monday morning, Chuck was relieved to see Dennis alive, standing by Chuck's Chevy in the driveway as usual, but worn-out looking, with tired eyes.

"Where in the hell have you been?" said Chuck. "*Damn*, you're smelly, too. What in hell happened to you?"

"You ain't gonna believe this, Charley."

"Okay, I'll give you some time," Charley said, folding his arms and leaning against the fender.

"Saturday night I was drinking with the boys—you remember, we were giving you shit for being locked up. Anyway, I was getting on pretty good with it when it started getting real cold out. All I had on was a T-shirt, and I was shivering and getting sleepy. So, I saw this station wagon parked in the motel lot with its rear window down. I figured the owner was at the motel for the night. Peeking in, I saw a sleeping bag so I thought I'd take a little rest and warm up at the same time."

"So then what happened?"

"I woke up with a terrible headache, sun in my eyes. I reared up to find I was riding with a couple I'd never met. The driver shrieked and nearly ran off the road. He was scared shitless and so was his wife. I was scared, too. I couldn't remember then how I'd gotten in the car. And I didn't know where I was."

"What'd they do?" laughed Chuck.

"The guy pulled over and I bailed out and started walking the way we'd come and didn't look back. About a mile down the road, I reached a sign that said 'Pendleton, 10 miles.'"

Chuck grinned. "That's hundreds of miles from here!"

"It sure is. I thumbed a couple of rides."

"Why didn't you call your folks?" Chuck asked. "They were worried!"

"I didn't have any money. I'd spent it all on beer Saturday."

"Get in, Dennis," he said, still laughing.

Chuck was never locked in another jail cell.

# 8

# GREETINGS

In February 1967, soon after his eighteenth birthday, Chuck received his notice to appear for a draft physical in Portland in July. Chuck was excited. Mom was worried. The Vietnam War was in the papers every day and she didn't want her only son being any part of it.

Dad recommended the Navy Seabees. "You'd like it, Charley. You'd be good at driving heavy equipment and learning about construction." The Seabees built airstrips, bridges, and every other conceivable thing needed to run a war on any continent. If bullets started flying they were trained to drop their tools and take up guns to defend themselves.

"Yeah, Dad," he said, thinking, *Who wants to be shot driving a road grader?*

In July, after arranging time off with Mr. Farley, Chuck took the Greyhound loaded with other boys across the state to Portland, where they unloaded at a building downtown. Inside, Chuck soon found himself shivering naked on cold concrete lined up with about seventy-five other boys. The doctor found him physically and mentally eligible to serve in the armed forces.

Dressed again, Chuck and the others were led to a row of recruiters sitting behind green metal desks ready to sign up anyone who was feeling patriotic. The crowd at the Navy recruiters' table was so large Chuck was spilled over in front of the marine recruiters. One of them, a big son of a bitch, glowered, stood up, and bellowed at him, "You little fucker, get over there with the rest of the women!"

*He's daring me to become a marine. Dad was a marine. He'd be proud of me.* "I'd sign up right now," he told the recruiter, "but I'd hate missing deer season."

"When's deer season?" asked the recruiter.

"September."

"I can bring you in on the delay program. You won't have to show up until sometime in October."

"Can I fly?"

"If you sign up for four years, I can guarantee you'll be in aviation. Whether or not you'll fly is up to you." He slid a ballpoint pen and a form across the desk.

The first question in bold letters stared up at Chuck: "Do you swear you have no criminal record?" Chuck hadn't expected this but didn't blink as the file cabinet at city hall flashed in his mind. But, oh well. He picked up the pen and checked the box.

Back on the bus, Chuck worried all the way home. He'd have to get to his juvenile officer before the Marine Corps did. He hoped Vandenberg would tear up his records when he told him he'd joined the Marines and would be gone a few years.

Vandenberg, smiling behind his desk, said, "So, you joined up, huh, Charley? That's great."

"Sure did, sir," said Chuck. "I'm going to be a marine. I got a problem, though."

"Oh yeah?" said John, raising an eyebrow. "What's that?"

"They won't let me in if I got any criminal records on the books."

"Well, you got some." Vandenberg pointed at the file cabinets.

"That's what I'm wanting to talk to you about."

"You show me the papers, and if they're real, I'll clean out your files."

Chuck laid the paperwork on the desk.

Vandenberg dropped his glasses down on his nose, leaned forward, and read. He grunted a couple of times then rolled his chair back and smiled. "You can consider it done, Charley, and congratulations." He rose from his chair and stuck out his hand. "You be careful now, hear?"

Chuck shook his hand, relieved. "Thank you, sir."

Feeling a foot taller, Chuck went home and told his parents he'd joined the Marine Corps. Dad's face turned red. "You're out of your mind!"

Shocked, Chuck said, "But you were a marine. I thought you'd like it."

"I know what you're getting into."

Mom was quiet. Chuck was unsure. He left for the dealership to find out how Jim Farley was going to take it.

Farley was standing behind the parts counter. "Hi Charley, how'd you like grabbing your ankles?"

"I'm joining the Marine Corps and will have to leave right after deer season."

"Marines, huh? What are you, crazy?"

"That's what everyone's been telling me."

# 9

# HARDTOP RACING WITH THE GOOD OL' BOYS

After high school graduation, Chuck worked full-time at the garage, adding more talents to his résumé: replacing mufflers, fixing brakes, and becoming the driver of the dealership's stock car, a souped-up 1955 Ford sedan.

Small towns in southern Oregon and northern California sported stock car racetracks. They were dirt ovals, mostly quarter mile. They ran races through the summer on Friday and Saturday nights. Lakeview's track carved into a hillside just outside of town. It was handy for the locals to sit on the hillside and cheer on their favorite drivers while getting dirt in their beer.

Chuck thought it was pretty cool racing hardtops, especially since he was only eighteen.

The garage mechanics called themselves "the crew" on race day, and kept and maintained the car, which ran a later-model V/8, a 312 police interceptor borrowed from a T-Bird. They had gutted the interior, leaving only the windshield, a bucket seat with a lap belt, and a roll bar made out of two-inch galvanized water pipe painted white. They'd disconnected the right front brake, added a weight jack, and chained down the left front spring, all for cornering, so the little Ford could stick to the dirt as Chuck roared it around the track.

Chuck was a quick learner, a fearless driver, and knew what the other driver was going to do before even he knew it. Chuck was a natural, and he and the crew soon began winning races in Lakeview and the other towns—and got noticed by other racers, good ol' boys around the circuit. They didn't take kindly to this young punk taking their trophies back to Lakeview.

They began to team up against Chuck, one in front of him and one on the side, boxing him in so he couldn't pass. It kept him from winning, and he didn't like it much. He knew he had the better car and drove as well as any of them. He decided if they were going to play rough, he'd show them how.

The next race was Saturday night at Alturas, a little town across the border in California. Chuck got off to a good start, winning the trophy dash. But when he got into the main event the boys boxed him in. Around they went like that, until the guy on his right front fender spun out, leaving room for Chuck to slip between the cars. Just as Chuck was trying to pass the car in front of him, the driver slammed into him, trying to block his escape. Chuck didn't let up and they drove into turn three like that, trading paint, until Chuck hit the gas, cranked the wheel to the left, and, using his rear fender, bumped the guy good, sending him into the corner sideways, up the banked turn, where he hit the wall and bounced over it, landing upside down in the pasture.

Chuck won that race. But, thanks to the good ol' boys, he was black-flagged for "racing brutality." He and his crew loaded up the car without the purse and headed for home. But it was a happy trip back to Lakeview, because they'd shown the good ol' boys they weren't so good after all.

Fall was coming, the season was over, and so was Chuck's racing career, but deer season was about to start. Chuck was excited about the hunt and was looking forward to being a marine. But he was sad he would have to say goodbye to Jim Farley, who'd been so good to him.

Chuck found him on the lot. "I guess it's time for me to quit now, Mr. Farley. I'm going to hunt deer for two weeks and then I have to report to San Diego. Could I get paid up?"

"Follow me into the office, Charley—how many hours you got?"

Chuck told him. In the office, Farley wrote a check and handed it over.

"This is a lot more than you owe me, Mr. Farley."

"You've been a good worker, Charley. I'm paying you through deer season."

"Jeez, thanks, Mr. Farley." Wow! A two-week paid vacation. Pretty good for a kid.

"Good luck, Charley, and remember your job will be waiting for you when you come home."

It was a great feeling to have a send-off like that.

## 10

# FROM BOOT CAMP TO VIETNAM

**C**huck bagged a forked-horned mule deer. But sadly, he wasn't going to be home to enjoy Mom's home-cooked venison feasts. Little did he know what that venison would do for him and his marines later on in Vietnam.

The big day came, October 18, 1967. Chuck said his final goodbyes and boarded a bus for Klamath Falls, where he flew with other recruits to San Diego. From there they were bussed to MCRD Camp Pendleton.

"Over here, you long-haired girls!" hollered the gunnery sergeant. "Your mothers aren't here. I'm your mother now!" The sergeant marched the sixty recruits of Delta Company into a barracks, where Chuck slept a moment before he was shouted awake.

In the dark, he was lined up on the parade grounds and herded to the barbershop for his one-minute buzz. Coming out, he was not a long-haired girl—he was one of sixty identical Delta Company recruits of the US Marine Corps.

Chuck realized why everyone had told him he was crazy for joining the Marine Corps.

The first couple of weeks were a mental and physical hell until Chuck made sense of it. It helped that he was in excellent physical condition from running up and down the mountains around Lakeview, whose downtown was five thousand feet above sea level. Camp Pendleton was right on the ocean. Chuck had never breathed air like that before. With that air Chuck could run like a deer all day and never tire. He was beginning to enjoy boot camp, though he was bummed that his name was the same as the enemy. That's when he changed his name to Chuck.

Finally, Chuck was handed an empty rifle, an M14, and he loved it even though they wouldn't let him shoot it yet. He was taught everything about it from nomenclature to repair and cleaning. Then, because the body must condition itself over time to ward off fatigue and cramping, he was physically trained while holding the empty rifle, spending days snapping into sitting, kneeling, standing, and prone positions.

After six weeks of boot camp, Delta Company was sent to Edson Range for two weeks of rifle training. Chuck would finally get to shoot his M14.

His instructors were experienced riflemen who had returned from tours in Vietnam. They were stern and all business, but they didn't huff and puff and yell at the recruits. Chuck learned how to adjust the rear sight for windage and elevation from the one-hundred-meter line to the five-hundred-meter line. He shot offhand, sitting, and prone. He was trained in rapid fire, where he had to get rounds off within a certain time. Targets were scored from 1 to 10 with a bull's-eye being 10. Although Chuck did very well from all positions, he loved the five-hundred-meter line. To him, being able to place a bullet in the bull's-eye at that distance with an open sight was a memory not to be forgotten.

At the end of rifle training, there was a scored competition. During rapid fire, as he ripped off the shots, his adjustable sight loosened and dropped. His bullet holes looked like he'd drawn a line from the bull's-eye to the center bottom of the target, costing him points. But he still shot 236 out of a possible 250, qualifying him as expert and the high shooter of the class.

Sadly, rifle training was over for a while. Delta Company was sent back to Camp Pendleton, where Chuck and the rest of the recruits participated in a final brutal physical test. Chuck finished second out of sixty in the class and graduated from boot camp. He received his primary MOS (military occupational specialty) 0311, meaning "rifleman."

When Chuck went back home on furlough, his dad was openly happy and proud that Chuck had become a marine. Mom was still worried. Dennis had left for the Army by then, but his other friends were still around. Chuck went back to drinking, but he'd grown up some. He wouldn't be needing the file cabinet.

After thirty days of furlough, it was time for Chuck's basic infantry training and another goodbye. Mom was still worried and Dad was, too, but hid it better.

Back at Camp Pendleton, Chuck learned how to fire different weapons—M60 and M90 machine guns, bazookas—and then how to throw hand grenades.

Then he learned to survive a simulation of war—as close to war as the military dreamed up—going on overnight camps with forced marches, living off the land, eating what they could find, and sleeping in foxholes. Lastly, they crawled under concertina wire while live rounds whizzed close overhead.

During the five weeks of infantry training, the recruits were turned loose at times. Chuck and his buddies went on the usual excursions like the San Diego Zoo and Disneyland. The night before Chuck was scheduled for an 8 a.m. test to qualify for aviation training, two

buddies invited him on a jaunt to San Diego to get tattooed.

"You ain't catching me with one of those," Chuck
said.

"Come along anyway," one said as he laughed. "You
can watch and hold my hand if the pain is too great
for me."

Chuck thought it silly to get a big mean-ass tattoo, especially before seeing any actual combat, but
went along.

Before going under the needle, his buddies decided
to have a few drinks to brace themselves. Chuck went
along with that, too.

The next thing he remembered was waking up in
a movie theater between his sleeping buddies. "Where
am I?!" he shouted, then, seeing the tattoo on his arm,
"Where'd this come from?" then looking at his buddies'
arms, "Where's yours?" He was the only one who'd gotten tattooed. Looking at his watch, he said, "It's five a.m.!
I gotta be at the base for the test at eight."

Chuck flunked the test. He would have to wait a whole
month to take the next test, while working in the mess hall.

While washing dishes and being glum, he found out
about a new scout sniper program. The Marine Corps
hadn't had one at the outset of the Vietnam War, but
as things escalated, they'd developed it. Each infantry
regiment contained one scout sniper platoon, consist-
ing of three squads of five two-man teams. The scout

sniper squad leaders assigned the teams to companies and, as situations dictated, moved them in and out.

Because Chuck had qualified as expert in rifle training, he was offered a chance to enroll in the four-week scout sniper school. He loved shooting rifles more than being a pilot, so he entered.

Again, Chuck was blessed with good instructors— marines, mostly corporals, who had returned from real war in Vietnam. They started Chuck's sniper training with an overview of how the system worked in war. Upon reaching a scout sniper platoon in Vietnam, Chuck would begin as a spotter for a two-man team. During his time as spotter, he would learn the ropes from his team leader, an experienced sniper. When his team leader rotated back to the states, Chuck—with the blessing of his team leader and the sniper platoon leader—would move up to sniper. As a sniper, he'd be assigned a spotter.

Chuck appreciated knowing how the system worked and looked forward to being on a sniper team as soon as he reached Vietnam.

Next, the instructors taught Chuck skills by throwing in every war scenario they could think of. Chuck learned how to use and detect camouflage, smell out booby traps, and read a compass. Most important, he learned to know where he was in daylight and in pitch dark, because he'd need to know his location on the battlefield in case he had to call in artillery close to his own troops.

The simulated battlefield at scout sniper school was mapped in quadrants. Chuck and the other trainees were sent out at night to find certain quadrants that were guarded by marines posing as bad guys. A trainee's goal was to pretend-shoot the bad guy, then put his number in a box at the quadrant to prove he'd done it.

Then, at the rifle range, Chuck was handed a Remington 700: his first true sniper rifle. He was awed by the feel and balance. The Remington, equipped with a 3–9x Redfield scope, had been chosen by the USMC as their current sniper rifle. Little did Chuck know that the rifle he held in his hands was a copy of the rifle he would use to outscore all marine snipers before and after that moment.

Chuck learned how to use and maintain the rifle, and that its 308 ammo would interchange with the M14 and M60 machine gun. He learned to estimate distance: guess, then step it off. He practiced until he became proficient.

In addition to what he'd already learned rifle training, he learned to use DOPE (data on previous engagements) when sighting in the Remington. First, fire the rifle at the bull's-eye on a target at a certain distance. Next, record on a card how much the bullet dropped, and use that information to adjust the rifle sights to compensate for the bullet drop. Then scribe the information—DOPE—on the magazine for quick reference to adjust the sights when in a hurry.

At the range on qualifying day, Chuck kept hitting bull's-eyes. His instructor hadn't seen anyone who could shoot like that. Chuck shot the highest score of any trainee up until that time, either acing the 200-point score or coming very close.

On April 19, 1968, he graduated from scout sniper school at the top of his class.

Chuck was now ready for war: MOS of 8541, scout sniper.

In a commercial airliner filled with marines of all MOSs, Chuck flew from San Diego to Hawaii, then off to Okinawa. Over the ocean, the cabin began filling with smoke. The pilot announced that because of engine problems, they were making an emergency landing on Wake Island.

Looking down at the tiny island, Chuck worried it was way too small to land the big jet.

*What if we crash this thing? All this training I did for nothing.*

Fortunately, as the big plane descended, the island grew.

After changing to another plane, the marines flew on to Okinawa, where they spent the day getting vaccinated, then received their gear, starting with a duffel bag, then the stuff to put in it: a backpack, fatigues, T-shirts, boxers, socks, blankets, towel, entrenching tool, first aid kit, flashlight with red lens, Ka-Bar knife, canteen, toothbrush and paste, shaving gear, bar of soap,

toilet paper, insect repellent, Tabasco sauce to help dis-
guise the taste of C-Rations, poncho, poncho liner, writing gear, and, of course, a deck of cards.

Chuck was impressed with how much his duffel
weighed and worried about having to carry it halfway
across Vietnam and back.

Chuck had one night for a last party. He splurged it
in bars, cooling his nerves for what possibly lay ahead.

The final leg was on a C-130 cargo transport plane.
The marines got quiet, not knowing what to expect.

May 1968, the C-130 landed in Da Nang, the busi-
est airport in the world due to the war, with over 2,500
military operations a day.

Chuck followed the soldier ahead of him and stepped
from the plane onto the airstair, blasted by heat. It was
like walking into a crematorium. At the bottom, his first
step on Vietnam "soil," his boots stuck to the melted as-
phalt of the tarmac.

With their duffel bags shouldered, the planeload of
soldiers was led to who knew where, on the way passing troops going home who laughed and heckled Chuck
and the others for being FNGs (fucking new guys),
"fresh meat."

Chuck wished he were as happy to be there as they
were to leave.

He found himself lined up in full sun on the tarmac
with about two hundred other FNGs, waiting. Sweat in
his eyes, he watched military aircraft of every descrip-

tion land and take off. A helicopter flew over with a half dozen soldiers clutching a cargo net hanging from its underbelly. *That's terrifying*, Chuck thought. *Hope the hell I won't have to do that.*

A Marine Corps officer holding a clipboard began shouting names over the airplane noise, telling each marine what their Vietnam MOS was, and to what company they were to report.

"Chuck Mawhinney!" the officer hollered. "MOS 0311, rifleman! Lima 3/5!"

"Sir!" Chuck called. "My MOS is 8541. I was sent here to be a sniper."

"Mawhinney!" the officer yelled back, "the Corps doesn't need snipers! It needs grunts!"

Shocked and angry, Chuck had no choice but to follow the men of Lima 3/5, who were grouping on the heliport to be flown north to 5th Marine HQ at Phu Bai.

## 11

# FIRST DUTY

Approaching Phu Bai by helicopter, Chuck saw Lima 3/5's perimeter within sight of the bridge he'd be guarding. Inside the perimeter were tents, armaments, and stacks of supplies, all surrounded by foxholes.

Arriving in the perimeter, Chuck saw marines going about their daily routine like zombies, staring at objects Chuck couldn't see. Their uniforms were tattered and their boots had turned from black to light brown from the water they'd tromped through. Chuck's brightly polished black boots made him feel like a foreigner.

He was shown a tent where he stowed his gear. Then, as ordered, he lined up at supply for his in-country gear: grenades, C-4 plastic explosives, extra canteens, ammunition, and a new M16—a Mattel-looking gun that Chuck instantly disliked.

Back at his tent Chuck transferred some of his personal items from his duffel bag to his backpack for day patrol. That done, he glanced around for the latrines. Seeing none, he grabbed his entrenchment tool and took a walk.

Next morning, Chuck woke up to another day hotter than hell, and his thirst was maddening. At breakfast in the mess hall, he couldn't drink water fast enough. Then he had to go on his first patrol. It was the company's duty to guard not only the bridge but to monitor the area around it. As they moved through the area, Chuck spotted small green pineapples growing wild. Loving fruit, Chuck picked a few.

"Don't eat those," said his squad leader, Fofo Tuitele, a large Samoan man.

Chuck figured Fofo was probably kidding. What could be wrong with pineapple? Besides, his stomach was made of iron. So, he stored them in his backpack and walked on.

They entered a village, where some kids were drinking water from a bucket out of a well. They offered him the bucket—the water was cool. Chuck drank his fill, thanked the children, and walked on.

Back inside the perimeter, Chuck used his USMC Ka-Bar knife to cut the pineapples into slices and ate the wonderful fruit—a little sour but a great diversion from the C-Rations he'd been eating.

Soon, Chuck's stomach began to cramp. It hurt like hell and his bowels churned. He grabbed his entrenching tool and ran. After emptying his bowels, he began puking, something he was good at. This was worse, though. Chuck was on fire and thought he was going to die. He was suffering the curse of pineapples and tainted water. So, Chuck, the company's new boy, went through the agonies of diarrhea in front of God and everyone.

Later, he was on his knees next to his tent retching up nothing but memories. He heard someone say, "What's the trouble, Marine?" It was Fofo.

"I'm dying," Chuck moaned, wiping his face with the back of his filthy hand.

"You the guy who picked the pineapples?"

"Chuck Mawhinney," Chuck moaned, nodding his head.

Fofo gave Chuck a friendly pat on the back. "You ain't gonna die, but you'll wish you had before this is over."

Fofo carried clean water to Chuck and poured it down him. At first the water made Chuck cramp up, rolling like a contortionist and blowing it back up as fast as he swallowed it.

"You're killing me!"

"You can do it, Chuck. Just one more drink."

Fofo kept up the flushing through the night, until Chuck could hold some of it down. Then Fofo gave him pills for dysentery. The next day, Chuck began to think he might live.

"Thanks, Fofo," Chuck said, smiling. "I guess you saved my ass."

"You could say that." Fofo grinned. "Welcome back from the curse. But you're still in hell."

Chuck noticed a helicopter flying in toward the perimeter with a supply net hanging from its underbelly.

"Wonder what's in the net?" said Chuck.

"Hope some of it's mail," said Fofo. "I haven't got any for a while."

They watched the helicopter set the net on the LZ, hover while releasing the straps, then fly away. A corporal pawed through the net, dragged out a mailbag the size of a garbage can, and carried it to the center of the perimeter.

By the time Chuck and Fofo arrived, the marines had gathered around the corporal like he was Santa Claus. Holding up the first letter, he hollered out a man's name. The lucky marine pushed through the crowd and took the letter from the corporal like it was a treasure, smelled it, and, grinning, held it up like it'd been perfumed by his sexy girlfriend back home. Everyone cheered.

"Mawhinney!" the corporal called out, holding up a package. Chuck raised his hand. The corporal tossed it over the crowd to him. Chuck caught it tenderly, like it was a dozen eggs. It was the size of a shoebox wrapped with brown paper and tied together with string.

"Who's it from?" asked Fofo.

"From my dad," said Chuck. "I've gotten letters from him, but this is the first package. I wonder what's in it?"

"Open it." Fofo handed over his Ka-Bar. "Let's see what it is."

Chuck tore into it, handing the shredded paper to Fofo, and opened the lid to find a letter and strips of jerky wrapped in newspaper.

"It's deer jerky," said Chuck, biting off a hunk and holding the box out to Fofo. "Here, you'll love it."

Fofo tore off a bite with his large white teeth. "Wow! This is good! Where'd he get it?"

Reading the enclosed letter, Chuck said, "It's from the deer I killed right before I left for boot camp. Dad says he had the whole thing jerked and there's more coming."

"Good! This sure as hell beats C-Rats."

Chuck handed the box to the nearest man. "Hey asshole, take one of these and pass it on."

"Fofo!" the corporal yelled.

Back at Chuck's tent, sitting on supply crates, Chuck and Fofo, smiling, reread their letters. Fofo carefully folded his and slipped it into his pocket. Chuck put his in the empty jerky shoebox.

Fofo began to talk. "Chuck, you're going to be in-country for a long time. I've got some advice."

"I'd love to hear it."

"I'm going to tell you how to know trouble before it happens. Watch the people, Chuck. They will teach you. Watch their routine. Then if their routine is broken, there's a reason. Watch where they walk—if they're avoiding a trail or cutting a corner in a rice paddy, there's a reason. The Viet Cong like using booby traps but they also know and rely on the villagers. So, to protect them, they tell them the location of the traps.

"Don't play with things, Chuck. The Viet Cong knows Americans are curious. So anytime you see something you're not absolutely sure of, leave it alone. If it were safe, local kids would have already taken it. If it is there, it could be a booby trap. Americans like to kick cans and drag their feet climbing onto rice paddy dikes. Locals do neither. The reason is obvious."

Then Fofo taught Chuck to use his senses: "Use your eyes to tell your brain when anything changes. But first, you need to know what's ordinary. Look around. Don't just look at what you see, look deeper. The farmer is working alone with his water buffalo. Should there be other farmers there? Is it the season a farmer should be in the paddy with his buffalo? Is he focused on his work or hesitating and gawking around? What does the rice crop look like? Is it even, or are there places where it doesn't look normal for the season? How about the tree line behind the farmer? How thick is the vegetation in the tree line? Examine the foliage—does it look normal? Are the plants, banana leaves, and bamboo growing in their natural direction or are they bent over? Are birds flying away, or is there any other kind of disturbance in or near the tree line?

"Your sense of smell can save you. You have a young, large nose—now you need to learn how to use it. Learn to know the natural smells that surround you. The smell of burning bamboo, cooking meals in a nearby village. Learn what time people cook dinner. So, it's dinnertime, but you don't smell that distinctive smell when approaching a village—what's wrong? Could the VC or NVA be in the village disrupting the locals' routine? People emanate a body odor—the more nervous they get, the more odor. Sometimes a pungent smell will come from bad food or water. Any detection of a different smell could indicate something is amiss. Use your nose and pay attention."

Then Fofo spoke in a quieter voice, "Learn and know the sounds of everyplace you go. You've been using those young, big ears for pleasure more than defense. Everything and everyplace has a sound. The birds, lizards, frogs, and other wildlife have a routine and if they're disturbed they'll sound different. Learn to distinguish night sounds from day sounds. Listen for anything different. A village has the sound of the locals working, eking out a living in this war-torn poverty-stricken country. The sound of rice stalks beating on hand-woven bamboo mats. The murmur of chatting during daily activities. The occasional grunt of the Vietnamese potbelly pig. The crying of an infant and the laughter of children playing. If the enemy is near or in the village, these sounds change. Even Charlie makes noise—moving vegetation in the dark of night. The quiet, hollow *bloop* of a distant enemy mortar tube. Sound tells a story and could save your sorry young ass."

"Learn to use your sense of taste. It isn't to just enjoy lobster dipped in garlic butter, or the pickle in your third bite of a hamburger. You have smelled something strong and been able to taste it. Taste is a sense that your brain usually does not register unless something changes. Odors can make a slight change in taste. Understand your normal taste and be aware of changes.

"The sense of feel—it's important to a soldier because battles are often fought at night. Half the time it's pitch dark. You will need to feel what's around you. A flashlight would be nice, but dangerous, because Charlie would see you, too. For emergencies or to read maps, only use your light with a red lens. The sense of feel develops through normal routine, and also contributes to the other natural senses.

"Chuck," Fofo said seriously. "The big one—the sixth sense. Your instincts. Trust your instincts."

Chuck would soon have a chance to observe Fofo's sixth sense from center stage.

They were on patrol to check out a village. From the tree line across the rice paddy from the village, Chuck noticed the villagers were acting oddly. They were grouped together outside their huts and the kids were gone.

Fofo wore a worried face.

"What's going on, Fofo?" Chuck asked.

"I got a strange feeling about this," he said. "Something tells me something is wrong." Fofo took out his wrinkly old map and sat down. He used the map to plot artillery to the tree line adjacent to their position. He passed on the coordinates to his radioman, who in turn asked the closest artillery to ready for a possible strike.

Then Chuck, Fofo, and the rest of the patrol swept the south end of the area and started toward the village. Suddenly—*crack! crack!*—enemy AK-47 bullets were flying from the tree line Fofo had plotted, whizzing by close enough to shave the fuzz off Chuck's ears. Chuck couldn't see the enemy, just their muzzle flashes. He joined the fight, but his M16 jammed. Was this a suicide mission? He tried to unjam it on the run as the marines pulled back. Fofo radioed for the artillery strike he'd already plotted. Huge artillery shells whistled overhead and crashed into the enemy tree line not more than a hundred yards from the marines. The deafening explosions blew tree limbs apart and scattered the enemy.

No marines died that day. Chuck admired Fofo. How had he known to stop and move his men back? How had he known he was walking into an ambush? It was Fofo's sixth sense. His instincts.

But it was mind-boggling to Chuck to be in a war with a defective rifle. He tried everything; adjusting and cleaning, but it didn't help. Most other marines' rifles didn't jam, so Chuck knew he had the worst of the bad. He tried trading it at the armorer's tent but no luck.

From then on, Chuck trusted his own instincts but not his M16.

# 12

## THE REAL WAR

**A**fter that initiation, Chuck spent more than two months at the bridge as an M16-carrying grunt with Lima 3/5. He went out on patrol about three times a week, mostly to villages looking for any evidence of the Viet Cong or NVA. The villagers were friendly to the Americans—a sign that the enemy wasn't in the area anymore. Chuck began to wonder where the war was.

Meanwhile, the war was at a US Marine combat base located in the An Hoa Basin, twenty-five miles south of Da Nang. The basin was an agricultural region known for growing rice, fruit, and maize. So, it was a popular stop-off point for the communist NVA army on their way to fight the South Vietnamese army via the Ho Chi Minh trail. Some NVA and Viet Cong (also communists) had taken over civilian villages in Arizona Territory, Dodge City, and Go Noi Island. The villages were linked by hedgerows and trails, so they were easy for the communists to defend. The Viet Cong policed the area for the NVA and ratted on any local villagers who helped the Americans. With the threat of certain death, the locals handed over food and anything else the communists wanted. The Viet Cong posed as farmers in the daytime, then turned into combatants at night. In addition, the communists on Go Noi Island were harassing Da Nang with rockets and sappers. The An Hoa US Marine base had been built to protect the villagers and Da Nang. Marine patrols pushing back on Go Noi Island had set off a ferocious battle known as Operation Allen Brook.

Into his third month at the bridge north of Phu Bai, Chuck and the rest of Lima 3/5 were flown to An Hoa to help with Operation Allen Brook. The An Hoa base was larger and much more lively than the bridge that Chuck had been guarding. Planes and helicopters and trucks were coming and going, tanks clattering, Jeeps buzzing here and there. Little flatbeds called M274 Mules buzzed up and down the streets and alleys, carting around supplies and personnel.

As soon as Lima 3/5 checked in at An Hoa, they crossed Liberty Bridge with full gear to Go Noi Island to join Operation Allen Brook. Chuck entered the firefight carrying his piss-poor M16 rifle.

An M60 machine gunner fighting close to Chuck was killed. The machine gun assistant took over shooting duties, and Chuck became his assistant, feeding the belt and helping with transport. Then, that machine gunner was killed and Chuck found his hands clamped on the burning-hot handles of the big gun, spraying bullets at the enemy's position.

After the firefight, he realized he didn't know if he'd killed anyone or not.

Then he was told he'd be the permanent M60 machine gunner. Though he'd be rid of the M16, he knew the life expectancy of a machine gunner was short. Chuck tried to trade off the big gun but there were no takers.

During a pause in Operation Allen Brook, Chuck discovered Lima 3/5 was now outfitted with a scout sniper team. This was the first time he'd even heard the word sniper since being informed he wouldn't be one. It didn't take him long to introduce himself to Sniper Corporal Albury, who said he was based at a sniper platoon located at An Hoa, and he needed a spotter. Chuck had to get to the sniper platoon leader at An Hoa and request the position.

So he faked a toothache and was sent into An Hoa. He bypassed the dentist on his way to find the sniper platoon leader. He found him at the sniper platoon office, where Chuck convinced him he was the man for the job. The platoon leader cut orders for Chuck to transfer from Lima 3/5 to the scout sniper platoon, 5th Marines HQ. Chuck was so ecstatic his tooth quit hurting.

The platoon leader told him to report to the snipers' tent next door. It was a large tent, where he would live with eight sniper teams of two men each. Chuck was assigned a cot with space underneath for his duffel bag with personal items he wouldn't take to the field.

Chuck joined Corporal Albury as his spotter. Albury had only one mission left before he rotated home, so he moved fast, taking every opportunity to teach Chuck everything he knew about being a sniper besides just shooting people.

"Grab your backpack," said Albury. "We're gonna go see the armorer and get you outfitted for spotter."

The armorer tent looked somewhere between a sporting goods store and a jeweler's shop and smelled like gun oil and cigar smoke. Behind the counter that spanned the width, the armorer wore an apron and smoked a cigar.

Chuck handed over the M16. "Throw away this son of a bitch. It's never been any good and it never will be."

The armorer's eyes narrowed but he took the gun and leaned it on a rack alongside a hundred more just like it. Chuck wondered about those rifles—how many were defective and what had happened to the men who had used them? How many went home in body bags? Chuck felt sorry for the next bastard who'd own his.

Chuck finally had his M14, a real gun. He was in hog heaven. It was specially made for snipers: it was modified with very close tolerances so the barrel and stock couldn't jump around and it was equipped with a folding bipod. The windage and elevation adjustments were sharp and crisp, unlike the worn-out one he'd used in training. He couldn't wait to "sight it in."

"How many twenty-round clips you need?" asked the armorer.

"Five," Chuck said, remembering training.

"He wants six," Albury said. Then to Chuck, "They're used clips, so later you'll want to sort through them for the best five. Tape two clips together, one up and one down so then when you're in a hurry all you'll have to do is flip them."

Cradling the clips in his arms, Chuck said, "This doesn't seem like much ammo for thirty days."

"Getting more ammo for the Remington is just a radio call to HQ," said Albury, "and any company we're assigned to will have ammo for the M14. Also, even though the M14 ammo will fit the Remington, it varies in size and load, so never use it unless it's absolutely necessary.

It's also very important to never use a company's tracer rounds in the Remington, because they tend to wear on the precision-made barrel."

Next, Albury took Chuck to the supply tent.

To his already heavy duffel bag Chuck added a set of camouflage fatigues, four pairs of green socks, three green T-shirts, three pairs of green boxers, a shoulder web, field glasses, a starlight scope with spare battery and smoked lens, rifle cleaning rod and cleaning brush, Hoppe's solvent and gun oil, and rubber bands made from car-tire inner tubes.

For carrying on his body, Chuck was given a green handkerchief for cleaning his rifle lens and wiping sweat from his eyes, a compass, and a topographical map.

Before Chuck could pocket the map, Albury flattened it on the counter and showed Chuck the areas he'd been in and the areas they might be going. Albury warned he wouldn't be happy any time Chuck couldn't point on the map exactly where they were.

"By the way," Albury said, "we're pulling out in the morning."

"Where we headed?"

"We're assigned to Alpha 1/5 for thirty days, in the An Hoa Basin."

"How do you know that?" Chuck asked.

"This morning I checked the 5th Marine assignment board in the sniper office. We'll go over our gear tonight and catch a ride out tomorrow on their supply bird."

# 13

# SPOTTER

**E**arly the next morning, Chuck and Albury had breakfast in the An Hoa mess hall. It was the last "home-cooked" meal they would have for a while. Chuck filled up on meat, potatoes, and eggs, and drank all the cold milk he could hold. All cameled up, Chuck and Albury sloshed to the snipers' tent to gear up. Chuck grabbed his M14 off his backpack and lifted the pack by its shoulder strap, amazed at how much more it weighed with the added sniper gear. Outside the tent, he slung his pack onto his back and followed Albury to the airstrip to catch a ride to Alpha 1/5 company.

On the tarmac they found a crew loading a cargo net with supplies for Alpha 1/5.

"Now," Albury told Chuck, "we just wait for the supply copter."

"Think they'll let us on?"

"We're snipers, so we have a sure ticket. They see this Remington and they'll let us on even if someone has to get off."

Chuck was liking being on a sniper team.

Smoking cigarettes, they rested on their packs in the shade of an airplane wing, within sight of the loaded cargo net.

Hours later, a CH-46 twin-rotor helicopter arrived to pick up Alpha 1/5's supplies. Chuck and Albury heaved their gear in and jumped on. The crew hooked the cargo net to the bottom of the helicopter by long straps. As the helicopter ascended, the straps became taut and the bundle hung several feet below the craft.

Later that morning, the helicopter landed near the perimeter of Alpha 1/5. Albury and Chuck went looking for the CO to get introduced and ask what they'd been called out for.

"We've been having trouble with sappers at night," said the CO. "We want you guys to set up on the perimeter so you can do some business with 'em after dark. But until then, the day is yours."

It was a fairly secure area, so Chuck was able to shoot

and "sight in" his new M14. He zeroed in the rifle at one hundred yards, then measured bullet drop every hundred yards out to five hundred, writing down elevation changes for each distance. With his Ka-Bar knife, he marked one-hundred-meter DOPE on the gun's sight adjustment.

That evening, Chuck and Albury began their watch together in a large dark foxhole on the perimeter, listening to the night sounds of crickets and frogs.

Albury began passing wisdom onto Chuck, who listened to every word.

Albury whispered, "A sniper team spends a lot of time together—in fact, *all* their time together. They will and should get to know each other well. They'll know how the other is going to react in any situation. In most cases, the team stays together until the team leader ends his tour and goes stateside.

"However," Albury continued, "a team that functions well together can begin to feel comfortable; a false sense of security can creep in. Young and gung ho, the team takes more risks and gets a lot of kills and a reputation for being the 'bad boys.' The sniper quits teaching his spotter, they get lax, and the odds of being compromised increase. Because of that, the platoon leader will split them, sending the spotter to a different team and giving the sniper a new spotter. This is not all bad. If the new spotter is fresh from sniper school, he'll bring new training techniques. If the spotter is seasoned, he'll remind the sniper to revisit practice. Not just shooting practice, but range estimation, hold-offs, and observation skills."

Chuck was impressed by all Albury knew and thankful he was willing to share it.

Chuck and Albury finished the night in the foxhole without incident. In daylight, near the foxhole, Albury continued Chuck's on-the-job sniper training. "Sometimes you'll need to kill the enemy in the dark. In fact, *many* of your kills will be after dark. NVA and Viet Cong like to operate at night. Sappers sneak up on marines in the dark on suicide missions. Sometimes they'll spend three or four hours crawling the length of a football field, dragging with them a canvas satchel filled with some kind of high explosives with the intent of throwing it into the perimeter. Sometimes, on a calm night, you can smell 'em. They stink of death, shit, and urine mixed with the sweet smell of opium and marijuana. If they don't hit a mine or get caught in concertina wire, someone with a nightscope better take them out or there will be dead marines come morning."

*This is getting real,* Chuck thought. *I'm going to kill someone soon.* He remembered Sunday school: *Thou shalt not kill. How will I feel after I do?*

"To make these nocturnal kills," continued Albury, "you'll need to be proficient with the nightscope. I'm going to show you how." From his pants pocket, Albury pulled out a C-Ration box, about six inches long by three inches wide and one inch thick. "This will make a good target. It's full, so it will stay where we put it. Come with me."

Chuck followed as Albury stepped off a distance of seventy-five yards out of the perimeter into an open field, where Albury placed the box on the ground.

Back at the foxhole, Albury took Chuck's M14 and attached the bipod to it. He then assumed the prone position, rested the gun's bipod and butt on the ground, and put his eye to the peep sight. "Now I'm adjusting the sight until I'm looking directly at the center of the box." Albury rose, leaving the rifle frozen in place. "Let's have the nightscope."

Chuck handed it over like it was a newborn baby.

Albury pointed at the scope's dark lens. "This is the protective smoke lens for daytime shooting. Never take it off in the light or the scope will burn up. Next I'm going to attach the scope onto the rifle and adjust it, so it will also be sighted on the box."

Chuck watched close as Albury, without moving the rifle, attached the scope to the barrel then returned to prone position. Albury told him, "I'm turning on the starlight scope and adjusting the reticle to the center of the box." He rose and backed away. "Now you take a look."

Chuck dropped to prone and peered through the scope. The C-Rats box and everything else was bright green like new grass and blurry. "Wow," Chuck said. "Will it look like this after dark?"

"Pretty close, depends on if there's starlight or moonlight. The more light, the better the scope will pick up shiny objects, like an enemy's face. If it's pitch dark, you're shit out of luck. Recheck the peep; make sure it's still dead-on."

"Perfect," said Chuck.

"Whenever you know you'll be on night duty, use this method to make sure the reticle is in the same position as the peep sights, and you'll be good to go. Now turn off the scope. We're going to the CO and get permission to take a practice shot tonight, an hour after dark."

Permission was given for one shot, and the word was passed around the command post and up and down the lines.

In the foxhole, an hour after dark, Albury asked Chuck to find the C-Rats box and take the shot. Chuck put his eye to the starlight scope. The whole world was lit up, fuzzy green. He searched this new world for the C-Rats box, found it, and shot.

"Hit!" Albury said.

"But I didn't see it move."

"Oftentimes the spotter will see more than the shooter. So when the bullet impacts Charlie, say 'hit.'"

The next morning, they walked out to examine the C-Rats box. To Chuck's surprise, it had a bullet hole near its center. He hadn't seen the hit before because of the scope's blurred vision. Now he was even more confident of himself and what he could do with his M14.

A few days later, Chuck and Albury were told they'd be going with Alpha 1/5 on foot into Arizona Territory to find NVA buildup. Chuck knew the reputation of the Arizona, so named because of its shoot-outs, reminiscent of the old American West. Dangerous country where you either killed or were killed.

The next morning, Alpha 1/5 departed.

With Chuck's first step on the trail into the Arizona, he sensed trepidation falling like a fog over the column of grunts. *Am I about to die?* He became super alert, walking on the balls of his feet, M14 at the ready.

The marines liked to keep their snipers alive, so Albury was midway in the column and Chuck ten yards behind him. Ten yards behind Chuck was the radioman. At the front of the column was the point man. His job was to lead the company through booby traps, mines, and enemy troops. Point men used their instincts, like Fofo had taught Chuck. Point men were brave beyond any imagination. If they weren't killed right off, they were very good at what they did.

Looking ahead, Chuck saw the column of marines enter a village, snaking through the huts like a serpent stalking its prey. Chuck entered the village. The place was quiet as if vacated. Chuck felt eyes on him as he passed darkened doors of empty huts. He whispered ahead to Albury. "What's up?"

"The villagers are underground," Albury whispered back. "They're in bunkers left over from the war with the French. It's America's war now, but still the same death and destruction."

Chuck wondered how the villagers managed to survive with the NVA and Viet Cong stealing their food.

AK-47s erupted; the column jumped for cover, crouching between huts.

"Snipers up!" The yell came back through the line.

Chuck raced after Albury through a hail of bullets past the hunkered-down marines until at the village edge they found the CO on his knees, surrounded by grunts firing M16s across an open field and into a tree line about one hundred yards distant. The radioman slammed down next to the CO, who was scanning the tree line with field glasses. "Get An Hoa!" the CO yelled over the mayhem. "I'm calling in a strike!"

The radioman got busy, "Come in, An Hoa! Come in, An Hoa! Over!" while the CO's outstretched fingers itched to get the radio.

"What can we do?" hollered Albury.

The CO yelled back, "Point man is shot and down, in that open field about twenty yards from the enemy! Charlie's got him in his sights! Every time our guy moves, the asshole shoots him again! We've got to get him off our man!"

Chuck and Albury quickly found an opening in the brush close by where they could see the point man and the tree line beyond. The point man was crying in pain as the bullets whizzed over him back and forth. Chuck and Albury frantically glassed the tree line for the shooter tormenting him.

The point man tried to get up—*thud!* Another round hit him in the body.

"We ain't got much time," Albury said. "Charlie will finish him off soon."

Overwhelmed with grief for the point man, Chuck asked, "Why doesn't Charlie just kill him? Put him out of his pain?"

"The motherfucker's playing with us," Albury said. "He's daring us to come out for our marine. Then he'll take us out one by one."

From the corner of his eye Chuck saw a marine with a shotgun, crawling through the short grass toward the point man.

"Get back!" the CO bawled out.

"He's my best friend!" he shouted back, still moving. "I gotta get him!"

Chuck searched madly through his field glasses for the bastard who was cruelly executing a fellow marine right in front of his eyes. *Where the hell's that artillery strike?*

*WHACK!* Another round pounded the point man, jerking his head to one side. His body twitched in death. The point man's best friend stopped, turned, and crawled back.

"I see the son of a bitch!" Albury cried out. *CRACK!* his Remington spoke. "That fucker won't be shooting any more marines."

"Where was he?" asked Chuck.

"At the base of that large tree, straight out, shooting out of a spider hole." A spider hole was a man-size tunnel entrance with a camouflaged lid.

Chuck swung his field glasses toward the tree. "There's a man hunkered down to the right of the spider hole. He's wearing camouflage but if you look close you can see his face."

"I see him. He's a dead motherfucker."

Chuck stayed on the enemy's face as Albury aimed. *CRACK!* A hole appeared in the man's forehead as bloody brain matter burst from the back of his skull.

"Hit!" Chuck hollered. He wished they'd killed 'em sooner, saving their point man.

Artillery shells whistled close overhead; Chuck and Albury dove into the dirt as the bombs detonated the enemy's tree line, blowing stumps and branches hundreds of feet in the air, some falling close to them. Hugging the earth, Chuck heard jets racing in, dropping boiling red napalm, torching the remnants of the tree line. He felt heat off the molten jelly that engulfed everything in its path. Chuck was horrified by the smell of burning human flesh.

He heard helicopter rotors and, looking up, saw a pair of olive-green angels appear overhead. They settled into the LZ close to where the dead point man lay under a poncho. The sight of the savaged marine infuriated Chuck all over again.

Chuck jumped in to help run the stretchers of wounded marines to the helicopters, then watched as the point man was carefully loaded and sent on the first leg of his journey home.

Then it was quiet. No animal noise. No one talked. Until the CO called the area secure: the air attack was over.

While Chuck and Albury scanned for escaping NVA, the grunts entered the smoking aftermath, looking for survivors. They found only twisted gun barrels, spent ammunition, and smoldering corpses.

# 14

# CHUCK'S FIRST KILL

Chuck and Albury led the CO through the hellish scene to confirm Albury's kills. The enemy soldier slumped in the hole with his hair burnt off and a bullet hole between the bridge of his nose and one eye.

They searched nearby for the second kill. Chuck pointed with his cigarette. "He *should* be right here."

"Well, he ain't here now," the CO said.

"I saw him go down," Chuck insisted. "Albury hit him hard; he was dead before his chin hit the ground."

"Big guns and bombs and napalm turned him to ash," the CO said. "Then the wind blew him all the way to hell."

Albury pulled out his book of kill sheets and a worn-down pencil. He licked the lead and filled out two sheets: one probable, and one confirmed with the CO's signature.

He was a lot more than *probably* dead, but Chuck knew the rule: you have to have a body.

A few days after the point man incident, Chuck and Albury were called to assist Alpha 1/5 on a search-and-destroy mission. They were in the middle of the column, passing through a brushy area close enough to a large village they could see the huts.

AK-47s opened up from the village. Chuck ran after Albury through a barrage of bullets to find a shooting position at the village edge, passing marines who had spread out, advancing. Albury ducked behind a six-foot-wide pagoda and Chuck fell in beside him. The shooting died down. On their knees, peering from different sides of the pagoda, they scanned the area for enemy soldiers. The village looked empty.

"*Damn!*" said Chuck. "We're not gonna get a shot. Where'd they go?"

"They slipped out the back of the village. That's what they do. They hit us, then disappear."

Just then, an NVA darted from a big hut on the far side of the village and dove into an underground bunker. "I just saw Charlie," Chuck said.

"Where?"

"He jumped into a bunker about three hundred yards out to the left of the large hut."

"Shit, I'm looking at fifty huts."

Chuck watched close. Suddenly the man's head appeared, just a speck from that distance.

"He's right there."

"I can't see him."

"He's looking right at us. Look close and you'll see his face."

"He's hidden from me. Shit! *You* shoot the son of a bitch!"

They traded rifles. The Remington felt natural in Chuck's hands, like no time had passed since he'd torn up the targets in San Diego.

He rested the barrel on the pagoda and leveled the reticle on the man's face. Between heartbeats, he pulled the trigger—didn't feel the recoil or hear the shot—and watched the man die, the bullet piercing his forehead, blood gushing from his mouth as he blew over backward.

"Hit!" Chuck heard himself say, a habit from being spotter. *Thou shalt not kill.* But he just had. But he'd done it humanely.

"Are you sure you got him?"

"I've never been so sure in my life."

After the shoot-out ended and the area was secured, Chuck led Albury to the bunker, where the dead man lay on his back in the darkness. They dragged him up into daylight. There was a bullet hole between his eyes.

Chuck pointed at the corpse. "Thou shalt not kill my fellow marines."

"He's an officer," said Albury.

"How can you tell?"

"The insignia on his shirt. And he's heavier than most NVA, which means he's been eating well. And he's got this fancy pistol," he said, pulling an automatic from the body.

"That's a badass weapon," said Chuck. "Look! It's got a red star engraved in the grip. He's a communist. And the gun's mine—I made the kill." It was okay with the marines to keep enemy weapons as mementos.

"Russian made," Albury said, lighting a cigarette with his Zippo. "They're common," pocketing his lighter, "I've seen a lot of 'em. Never bothered to keep one, though. How 'bout you let me have this one—I'm going home soon and you'll get plenty of 'em."

Feeling obligated to Albury, Chuck said, "Well . . . okay."

Smiling, Albury stuffed the gun in his belt.

Chuck would come to regret his generosity. He would never see another gun like it in all his three tours in Vietnam.

When Chuck and Albury returned to An Hoa, Chuck went straight to the sniper office to hand in his kill sheet, thinking, *I wonder how many more there will be?*

He found the platoon leader sitting on the edge of his desk and handed the sheet over.

"This says you got yourself an officer," said the platoon leader. "A rare feat—especially since this is your first kill. Got any evidence?"

"He's dead." Chuck pointed to the sheet where Alpha 1/5's CO had signed off on it.

"That's right. It's a confirmed kill. I'll start you a file."

Neither man knew it would become the biggest file in Marine Corps history.

Chuck, now confident—a man with a confirmed kill—returned to his peers in the sniper quarters.

## 15

## SNIPER

ext morning, Chuck woke and reached for his watch
he'd left on the ammo box next to his cot, but it wasn't
there. He jumped up, looking. It wasn't *anywhere*. He
hollered, "Where's my watch?!"

Albury laughed from the far end of the tent. "I for-
got to tell you about the monster rat."

"You shittin' me?"

Everyone laughed.

"No," Albury assured him. "Scout's honor. You lay
anything shiny down and he'll get it."

"I don't believe a word of it."

"It's true. He lives in the pallets under our feet and

when we're asleep or gone he collects watches. But if you don't believe that, you will believe the cockroaches. They're as big as roller skates and the sugar ants can haul your ass off."

*Maybe the rat does exist,* Chuck thought. He'd heard about rats living in mountains of garbage that surrounded bases. Not little like mice, but Vietnam rats— colossal rodents as big as cats with sharp teeth that cut through wire. An American garbage pile was a gourmet diet. A single pair of rats multiplied hundreds of times each year, yielding a horrifying number of the voracious creatures. Sometimes, sapper corpses were accidentally buried by bulldozers covering garbage piles with dirt. When monsoon rains eroded the piles, an occasional arm or foot popped up. Spotlights from the tower illuminated rats snapping and biting each other for the taste of rotting human flesh.

Chuck hoped he'd never see that spectacle while on night watch.

And as for the jewelry thief, much later Chuck would be told that when it came time to tear down the snipers' tent, the monster rat abandoned his cache of jewelry and ran for the shitters with the snipers giving chase wielding shovels and two-by-fours. The rat won the race and Chuck would never see his watch again.

Knowing Albury was going home in a few days, Chuck pressed him for more of his tricks of the trade. So, in a safe place near the base, surrounded by pagodas

shattered by war, Albury helped Chuck practice esti-
mating distances. Albury would point out a clay shard
and Chuck would estimate how many yards they were
standing from it. Then Chuck would pace it off to see
how close he'd guessed. His estimate was usually very
close.

Then they practiced shooting the clay shards that
surrounded the broken pagodas. The shards exploded
on impact. Chuck never missed.

"You're a natural," Albury said.

Immediately after Albury departed for home, Chuck
was called to the snipers' office.

"Chuck," the platoon sergeant said, "you've been a
spotter a very short time, but because of your perfor-
mance in the field and Albury's recommendation, it's
been decided that you will be made sniper team leader."

"Thank you!" Chuck said, not doubting they'd made
the right decision.

"Normally you'd get Albury's gun, but it was sent to
the armorer for a new barrel and reconditioning." He
handed Chuck a brand-new Remington 700.

Chuck was as surprised and elated as the day Grandpa
handed him the brand-new Red Ryder BB gun.

Chuck's first spotter, Wayne, was not only new to Chuck
but new to Vietnam. The lucky bastard had come

straight from sniper school. The man had not been tested. Chuck was wary. How would his spotter react to combat? Especially since they were going direct to Delta 1/5, for a month in the badlands of Arizona Territory.

As a newly minted sniper team leader, Chuck hoped for Delta 1/5's support on whatever sniper missions lay in store. Chuck knew what it was like to be a grunt. A Marine Corps company became like brothers; they trusted each other and were suspicious of an FNG until he proved himself—and if he didn't, he'd be sent packing. Chuck wanted to gain the confidence of the CO and the grunts. So, his goal was for his sniper team to become an important and respected part of the company as soon as possible.

As Albury had shown him, first thing on arrival at Delta 1/5, Chuck found the CO, introduced himself and Wayne, and asked what they could do for him.

"Sappers have been harassing us at night," the CO said. "They've been crawling close and heaving their homemade bombs at the perimeter. So far none have gotten in, but nobody's been sleeping too well—hope you can help get them off us."

"We'll set up with our nightscope on the perimeter," Chuck said, "and see if we can pop one of 'em for you."

After Chuck and Wayne made their ponchos into tents and stored their gear, they walked the perimeter from line position to line position introducing themselves to everyone in the company. The grunts were delighted to have a sniper among them. They showed Chuck from what side of the perimeter the sappers' attempts had been made. Chuck and Wayne carefully examined the area, finding small footprints on bare ground and where foliage was flattened like someone had dragged an object. A satchel bomb, Chuck guessed. The trails were scattered so it was difficult to predict just where the next sapper attack would come from.

Chuck located an open spot on a small rise about fifty yards out from the perimeter that offered a good place to spot anyone moving. Then they set up their night position on the edge of the perimeter as close as possible to the target area.

This would be Chuck's first real night of watching and waiting to kill an enemy combatant.

Chuck showed Wayne how to set up the M14 with the starlight scope, which was working well because of the cloudless night.

Chuck took the first watch with the scope, observing the bright green opening on the rise they'd picked out, waiting for the sapper to pass through. Chuck stared for about fifteen minutes, then, before his eyes began to trick him, he traded it off to Wayne.

While Chuck rested his eyes, he monitored the sensory of the night—tree lizards gabbing, frogs singing, mosquitos buzzing, fireflies flashing on and off in the vegetation, and the constant smell of burnt bamboo drifting in from distant villages—he waited for a warning, any sudden change from the norm.

Chuck and Wayne traded watch back and forth; the night seemed to go on forever.

After midnight, Chuck was monitoring the scope when the night sounds suddenly ceased. Chuck caught a glimpse of movement on the rise. He slipped off the safety. Within moments a green face appeared close to the ground next to a bush. Chuck squeezed the trigger; the sapper's face disappeared. The impact of the slug had spun the face away but Chuck could still see legs and a torso. They didn't move.

"Hit!" Chuck said it because Wayne couldn't see the sapper in the dark.

Chuck watched the opening for another sapper. Nothing for several minutes. A face showed. Chuck fired again. The bullet tore into the man's face, blowing the body over on top of the other. "Hit!"

After more minutes of waiting, the night sounds returned. The show was over.

The CO and a sergeant came to investigate. The CO asked Chuck, "What ya got here to show for two shots?"

Chuck pointed into the dark. "We got two dead, lying fifty yards out in an open spot."

"Damn, that's good," said the CO. "We'll take a look in the morning. I'm getting some sleep. See you at sunup."

Chuck and Wayne continued trading off watching

the area where the two dead sappers lay. Chuck was happy with the way his spotter was handling himself, but still wondered how he'd react when bullets blew both ways. Chuck was anxious for daylight when he'd see the results of his first shots as sniper.

The night dragged on.

Daybreak. Both corpses were in black pajamas, Viet Cong dress. The one who sprawled over the top of the other clutched an AK-47 and was dead from a bullet taken in the bridge of his nose. The other death-gripped a satchel of explosives and had a bullet through his right eye.

# 16

# LEARNING ON THE RUN

**B**y killing the two sappers that first night with Delta 1/5, Chuck had gained the respect he'd wanted of its grunts and the CO of Delta 1/5.

From then on, as he was assigned from company to company, all while training new spotters, he would never quit striving to earn the respect and appreciation from the grunts.

When assisting a company in-country, Chuck wasn't expected to do grunt's work. Some thought it too trivial for a sniper to get his hands dirty. Chuck wasn't that way. He earned his place among the company by doing things that would be noticed: when resupply flew in,

he helped carry and distribute the new gear; he volunteered to relieve grunts on night perimeter watches,
platoon-size night ambushes, and patrols.

On platoon-size patrols, Chuck had a hell of a time
trying to keep the grunts quiet and inconspicuous. They
seemed always in need of a smoke or to take a leak. But
bless their hearts, they would save Chuck and his spotters' asses on several occasions.

Meanwhile, Chuck was learning the habits of the
NVA and the VC. He could guess how they would react
when encountered. He shared these predictions with
COs, and, because of the respect they had for him, they
listened. He helped them plan patrols. Together they
went over routes and timing, and he would offer his
opinion and speculate on a patrol's outcome.

Then Chuck and his spotter would go out as far as
a thousand yards, searching for suitable hides for the
upcoming patrol and future patrols, spots that offered
vegetation from where they could watch for the enemy.
Finding them, they used terrain maps to figure out return routes to the company and establish coordinates
for meeting points in case they somehow got separated,
kind of like the James Gang planning a bank robbery.

On return to the company Chuck would meet with
the CO and platoon leaders to show the next hide's
position on the CO's map. This was to ensure there
were no friendlies in the area so Chuck and his spotter
wouldn't be caught in a cross fire. Then they'd establish

the time they'd depart and return so the grunts on the line would know when to expect them.

But no matter how much they planned, every trip out brought a different scenario depending on the weather, terrain, and enemy activity.

On one such occasion in the Arizona, Chuck and Wayne were returning from a hide, hidden from sight, when they passed a village and saw about a dozen VC opening bunkers where villagers hid, and then grabbing bags of rice from their arms.

Outnumbered, Chuck figured it would be suicide for him and Wayne to take them on themselves. They returned to the perimeter so Chuck could report the sighting.

"How many are there?" asked the CO.

"Hard to say," Chuck answered. "A dozen—maybe more."

"If we enter that village," said the CO, "they'll just shoot us up and then run out the back. You were there—you seen 'em, what do you suggest we do?"

"I'd say, just before dark this evening, Wayne and I set up in a hide where we can see the back of the village. First light tomorrow, send in the company. When bullets start flying the VC will turn tail and Wayne and I'll be ready for 'em."

"Okay!"

Chuck showed him the coordinates of the hide, and the CO passed the information to the company.

Just before dark, Chuck and Wayne set up in the hide under an overcast sky, a couple hundred yards from the village. From there, they could see both the opening where the marines would enter and the possible VC escape route out the back. There were no cooking fires in the village, no voices, no happy sounds. So Chuck figured the VC were still there.

The cloudy day yielded an especially dark night. Getting comfortable, they rested their backs against small trees, their legs stretched out in front of them. Chuck expected to spend a peaceful night taking turns with Wayne, watching and sleeping, even though he couldn't see a thing.

Sometime during the night, while Chuck was staring into the darkness, he felt something bump into his leg. *Whoa! What's that?!* Chuck couldn't see it in the pitch dark. But whatever it was, it was alive and moving over his leg just above the knee. It was heavy and cold and round like a giant hose. Chuck couldn't jump up and go screaming out of the hide—he'd wake up the whole village and all the VC.

It was okay to be scared of snakes in Vietnam. Boot camp drill instructors warned inductees that if they didn't get shot in Nam, they'd probably get bitten by a snake and die an agonizing death. There were over 140 types of snakes in Vietnam, many venomous. One of them was the "two-step" snake, so called because after it bites you, you can only walk two steps before dropping dead.

These horrific thoughts were going through Chuck's mind as the creature slithered over his legs on his way to where Wayne was sleeping.

Chuck poked Wayne.

"My turn for watch already?" Wayne whispered.

"There's a snake crawling over me," Chuck whispered through clenched teeth.

"You sure?"

"Hell yes, I'm sure. And he's heading for you."

"Fuck oh dear. It's on me. It's big."

"Yeah, and it's long. It's still on me, too."

Chuck felt the thing slither off him.

A moment later, Wayne wheezed, "It's gone."

The light of dawn dashed the memory of the snake; Chuck had bigger fish to fry. He swung his field glasses toward the opening of the trail where he expected marines to enter and made out movement in the morning shadows. The company's point man appeared in the opening, creeping along with another marine following ten yards behind. Good, Chuck thought. Things were going just like he and the CO had planned.

Wayne watched the grunts entering the village while Chuck scoped the VC escape route.

Shooting broke out on the other side of the village from Chuck and Wayne. Chuck figured the head of the column was in a firefight with the VC. With his sights on the escape route, he flicked the safety off.

Suddenly large-caliber rounds were hitting all around Chuck and Wayne. They went prone and hugged the ground as the hide rained broken limbs and branches. Chuck rose to his knees to see where the rounds were coming from. A grunt stood at the opening of the trail, an M60 cradled in his arms, spraying down the area around the hide.

"What's he shooting at us for?" Looking at Wayne, whose eyes were wide, Chuck felt hair rise on the back of his neck. He wheeled around to look behind him. VC were zigzagging toward them through M60 rounds, firing AK-47s from the hip.

"Come on!" Chuck ran with Wayne on his heels the two hundred yards to the cover of the huts while the M60 held the VC at bay.

The machine gunner saved their bacon that day. Luckily, he'd seen the VC sneaking up behind their hide, proving that preplanning works. Wayne learned and Chuck was reminded of a valuable lesson: don't get so intent on what's in front of you that you forget what might be behind you.

It was a nice cool day, cool for Vietnam anyway, when Chuck saw a helicopter approaching the perimeter. Chuck was curious what it was bringing. Mail? Cigarettes? Fresh water? Ammo?

The helicopter landed on the LZ. Two marines jumped out, neither wore a helmet, one had an M14, the other carried a Remington sniper rifle. *A sniper team!*

Camaraderie was high between snipers. Though it was not uncommon for a company to have more than one sniper team, Chuck rarely saw one outside of An Hoa, where he went only once a month.

Chuck called over to Wayne and they hurried out to welcome them. After introductions, Chuck and Wayne showed them where they could pitch their tents. The spotters got busy putting up the tents, leaving Chuck and Louie time to get acquainted.

"How's everything going out here?" Louie asked.

"We've been busy." Chuck pointed to a circle of huts built on a rise about six hundred yards away. "There was a shoot-out down at that village yesterday."

"You get a shot?"

"No, Wayne and I were in the wrong place—watching a trail—missed the whole thing. But it's secure now. The CO told me the VC are either dead or gone."

"Let's take a look," said Louie. "They might have left a souvenir, like a gun or something."

So Chuck and Louie slung their sniper rifles and started a leisurely trip down to the village while visiting and feeling a cool relaxing breeze on their necks. As they stepped through a tree line and approached the village, things seemed normal. Kids were playing, women were cooking and washing clothes. The village was calm. It seemed like the war had taken the day off.

But when they stepped into the village, it turned quiet. The villagers wouldn't look at them, then suddenly they were gone—disappeared like ghosts. Chuck and Louie raised their rifles and, back-to-back, scanned the area, expecting automatic rifle fire any second. Chuck knew they didn't have a chance with their long-bolt-action rifles and said, "It's time to leave." Louie didn't argue; they turned to run. AK-47s tore into the red dirt at their feet. Chuck and Louie sprinted through the tree line with VC on their tails and raced for the perimeter. About two hundred yards to go, they were met by their spotters and a squad of grunts, shooting back at the VC. When the VC saw the cavalry coming to the rescue, they lost interest and disappeared into the brush.

Chuck recalled another lesson: never, ever, leave your spotter and his M14 behind.

One evening, Chuck and Wayne were walking back to the perimeter, about eight hundred yards out, separated from the company by a hill. Chuck heard a helicopter overhead but ignored it; they were always on his side of the war.

They were moving through an opening past an old bunker covered with rotting sandbags, when Chuck saw it—a Huey gunship. Knowing it was a friendly, he still didn't think much of it. The Huey dipped, slowing down. It swung around and pointed its nose at them. Chuck saw rockets attached to its underbelly and M60s pointed at them. "Oh shit, we're in trouble!"

They ran and dove through a hole in the top of the bunker. The gunship fired a rocket that exploded close enough to shake the bunker, then opened up with the M60s, riddling the bunker's roof, cutting into the sandbags. Inside, the bunker was a mayhem of deafening noise, falling sand, and the smell of burning explosives as Chuck and Wayne lay facedown crowding the sandbagged wall. The roof began falling apart, drowning them in waves of sand. "I'm going to shoot the son of a bitch down!" Chuck hollered, but before he could get an aim on it, it stopped shooting and left.

Neither Chuck nor his spotter were injured. Madder than hell, with ears ringing and pockets full of sand, they made it back to the unit, where they learned that the companies' air support coordinator had saved them. Knowing Chuck and Wayne were in the area, he'd called the Huey off.

Another lesson learned: always hide from friendlies.

⊕

One night in the Arizona Territory, Chuck made a plan with the CO of Delta 1/5 to snoop on a village that the company was going to search the next day. Like many times before, Chuck and his spotter would leave before daylight and set up a hide about a thousand yards out from the company, close enough to observe the village. They would return after dark.

Before light, from inside the hide, Chuck and his new spotter Bill lay motionless and alert, the dawn rising in the east, about to wake the world to another blistering day of Chuck's war. The murmur of awakening day animals began rubbing out the night sounds of owls, and frogs and other nocturnal beasts that slithered themselves into the coolness of the earth. Chuck watched the village appear out of the darkness as mosquitoes sucked his blood.

But then the animal sounds stopped. Human sounds came from the village, but not the normal sounds. Instead, clinking of metal, muffled voices, shuffling feet, like an army coming awake. Hundreds of NVA soldiers stood up, sending shivers down Chuck's spine.

"We ain't gonna take 'em on, are we?" Bill whispered back.

"That would be crazy. There's too many of them."

Sunlight reflected off black shirt buttons—the NVA was forming up to leave.

"We need to warn the CO," whispered Chuck, "and *now.*"

Chuck and Bill slipped out the back of the hide and crept through elephant grass until they were out of NVA eyesight. Then in broad daylight they ran across open country, taking the fastest route, the same route they'd used coming out in the dark, making no effort to conceal themselves, hoping speed could make up for lack of cover, leaping over rocks and brush like an obstacle race. With about five hundred yards to go, they came to a bomb crater too large to jump, so skirted it—and ran into a slew of AK-47 fire coming from a tree line. Ambush! They turned and dove into the crater, bullets zinging overhead. Chuck felt helpless—every time he raised up to shoot, the crater was sprayed with bullets. Hunkered down next to him, Bill blazed away with the M14 on full auto at invisible targets. Chuck figured he and Bill were toast. No way were they going to get out of the crater alive.

Then from behind the AK-47s came marine battle cries and raging M16s. It was better than music.

Bullets stopped hitting the crater. Chuck raised up to see a squad from Delta 1/5 firing into the tree line. They'd come to the rescue. It was the marines: *Take the battle to the enemy.*

Soon as the area was secure, there was some thanking and hugging.

Chuck knew his efforts to quickly warn the CO had almost cost him and Bill their lives. The near disaster reminded him of his training: never return to the company on the same route as you left it. No matter how fast you run, you can't outrun a bullet.

# 17

# SUGAR BEAR

"**H**ey Bear, you wanna race me to the mess hall?" Chuck challenged his spotter from the snipers' tent in An Hoa. Sugar Bear was a huge Black man from New Jersey. Chuck figured he'd win easily since Sugar Bear outweighed him by a hundred pounds.

"Maybe," said Sugar Bear.

"Yeah," Chuck egged him. "I win and you burn my shitters."

"You sure you wanna do this, Mo?" Sugar Bear said. He called Chuck Mo for some reason Chuck didn't want to know.

"Yeah!" Chuck hollered out. "One, two, three—*go!*"

Sugar Bear left Chuck in a cloud of red dust.

Chuck couldn't believe he'd lost. Sugar Bear had ne-glected to mention he'd been drafted by the Philadel-phia Eagles before the war stole the opportunity from him. Chuck was stuck with his own shit-burning detail plus Sugar Bear's.

While Chuck was teamed up with Sugar Bear, his first monsoon season arrived, and the red dirt turned to mud. Chuck's feet were on fire with fungus inside his rotting boots.

The two were working with a company in the pour-ing rain, pitching up ponchos inside their perimeter, sticky mud everywhere, water running off the red clay to anywhere low. Chuck, not unbright, looked for high ground to set up their own poncho for the night. He spotted an old grave mound. Pointing, Chuck said, "Hey, Bear, let's put it up there."

Sugar Bear's eyes sparkled in agreement.

A grunt warned, "I wouldn't do it if I were you."

"Do what?" Chuck asked.

"Put your tent up there."

"Why?" Chuck said. "It's the best place here. High and dry."

The other marines snickered as Chuck and Sugar Bear erected their tent on the mound. Chuck figured they were just pissed that he and Sugar Bear got the best place.

At daybreak, Chuck woke up to a rat looking him straight in the eye. Startled, Chuck sat up. Horrified, he saw snakes, scorpions, and centipedes using his dry body for warmth. They were everywhere and on Sugar Bear, who was still sound asleep despite the pounding rain.

Chuck elbowed him.

"Huh?"

"Don't look down, just slip out of the tent."

"Why?"

Sugar Bear jumped straight up with the ponchos stuck to him like a folded umbrella. He tore himself loose, leaving Chuck sitting in the rain, throwing snakes, swatting centipedes, and relieved the rat had left on its own. Chuck heard guffaws and looked to see the entire company surrounding them, frozen and wet and bent over in hilarity.

Feeling foolish, Chuck and Sugar Bear broke down in laughter and everyone laughed and laughed.

Just after monsoon season, Chuck and Sugar Bear were sniping for a company of marines on Go Noi Island. After the company humped a trail all day, evening finally arrived. The company stopped and set up a perimeter hidden from the trail. Chuck and Sugar Bear were putting up their tent for the night when Chuck saw something odd about the vegetation nearby: some grass and a low bush were bent over.

Suspecting a land mine, Chuck inched closer to look. He spied a trip wire stretched two inches off the ground, just seven feet from where Sugar Bear was bent over driving in a stake.

"Bear! Don't move."

Sugar Bear froze.

"Land mine." Chuck stepped back to his pack and pulled out a roll of toilet paper to flag the mine. He tore off small pieces and carefully draped them over the wire.

He backed off and turned toward the company to yell for the engineers, but just then a marine came running up the trail. "Stop!" Chuck shouted but it was too late. The marine tripped the wire, igniting the bomb, which exploded, blowing both his legs to hell. Sugar Bear took the blast in his back, and it knocked him facedown onto the tent. "Medic!" Chuck yelled and fell to his knees next to Sugar Bear, who was howling in pain, his shirt blown away, his back shredded, oozing blood. Shrapnel—hunks of red-hot metal—stuck in his back from his waist to his neck. "Hang on, Bear! Help's coming!" Chuck looked over at what was left of the marine, who fortunately was unconscious.

A medic arrived in an instant, glanced at the unconscious marine, then dropped to his knees by Sugar Bear and began dressing his wounds. The CO and another medic ran up. That medic treated the other marine while the CO radioed for medevac, medical evacuation by helicopter.

Chuck felt blood running from the front of his shirt. He pulled off his shirt, surprised to see shrapnel had torn through his shirt and punctured the skin of his stomach area. His wounds were superficial so Chuck picked at them while waiting for the helicopter. The few feet he'd moved away from the land mine had saved his life. Chuck was thankful beyond words. But watching Sugar Bear and the other man bleed, he worried if the helicopter would arrive in time.

Chuck heard rotors coming, then saw the helicopter settle into a temporary LZ. Two grunts came running up the trail, bringing a stretcher for the unconscious marine. Chuck picked Sugar Bear up in his arms, carried him to the bird, and delivered him into the waiting arms of the on-board crew. The other marine was loaded, the helicopter took off, and both marines were flown to the military hospital in Da Nang.

Chuck worried about Sugar Bear for several months until they met up at An Hoa. It was a happy reunion.

# 18

# THE SCREAMER

**C**huck and his new spotter, Bill, were with Hotel 2/5, set up on Go Noi Island near a small village in the middle of a dangerous enemy area. To help out, Chuck had volunteered for night watch. Chuck and Bill had dug their foxholes deep for safety. It was still monsoon season, and it was an extremely wet and foggy night. Chuck's foxhole was filled with cold water from ground seepage and the constant drumming of the rain. Visibility was almost zero. His nightscope was useless.

To make life worse, later that night enemy mortar fire crashed into the perimeter—terrifying in the blindness of the dark. Then from the village came heavy

AK-47 fire, sending bullets low-whistling over Chuck's head. The marines sent up illumination flares but Chuck could see only a few feet toward the village. Then he saw muzzle flashes as the enemy advanced, and heard yells coming from fellow marines, "Charlie's breached the perimeter!"

Rule one when that happens: no one stands up. Anyone standing is considered enemy.

An Hoa artillery whistled overhead and hit close outside the lines. Illumination flares lit up the fog above the company as the enemy's small-arms fire cracked around them. Crouched in his foxhole, Chuck pulled out his .45, readying for a close encounter, straining his eyes for any movement.

Suddenly, an enemy soldier landed behind Chuck in his foxhole, screaming and stabbing him in the back, pressing him into the muddy wall face-first. Chuck twisted around and unloaded the .45. The screaming and stabbing slowed but didn't stop. Frantically Chuck forced another clip into his pistol, ready to blast away again. An illumination round went off directly above him, revealing the badly shot-up body lying in the water getting its dying kicks.

It was a large Vietnamese potbelly pig.

Apparently the animal had broken free of his pen in the village during the attack and had run wild until he'd stumbled in with Chuck, kicking and squealing in fright.

Chuck suffered from bruises, scrapes, and harassment from Hotel 2/5.

From then on, Chuck and his fellow marines referred to the battle as "Pork Chop Hole."

# 19

# THE MAN
# WHO FLEW

Chuck was walking on a wooded trail in the middle of a column of marines on a regular search-and-destroy mission, when he heard a commotion ahead and hurried to the front where he found the CO and other marines surrounding the entrance to an underground bunker.

The point man was telling the CO, "I surprised them, sir. They jumped across the trail in front of me, then headlonged into this bunker."

"So you think they're still in there?"

"Sure do, sir. Unless they snuck out the other end. Wanna smoke 'em out and shoot 'em, sir?"

"No," said the CO. "Let's smoke 'em out, capture 'em alive, and get 'em to talk."

That sounded good to Chuck. Information about the enemy was sparse and valuable. When Chuck saw an enemy up close he'd already killed him, so the enemy couldn't talk if he wanted to. Chuck pulled his .45, readying for a shoot-out just in case.

The point man yanked the pin on a smoke grenade and tossed it into the opening. The grenade clanked on the bunker's floor, followed by a muffled explosion. Acrid smoke erupted from the entrance. Coughing and choking, the enemy tumbled from the entrance. They came to their knees with their hands reaching high. A marine tied their wrists behind their backs and blindfolded them with white rags. They quieted, scared— sure they'd be shot.

Skinny, starved-looking prisoners, squatting in their dirty khaki shirts, shorts, and homemade sandals, they were easy to feel sorry for. But Chuck had no illusions. He knew they hated him. Just like he hated them. He and the rest of the marines knew if the tables were turned the little bastards would kill all of them—and wouldn't be nice about it, either. Chuck knew they'd make a special event of killing him, the one with the long gun. They would cut him up and dissect him and watch as he died a horrible death.

With the marines was a South Vietnamese Army interpreter who'd come along to communicate with villagers. He attempted to question the prisoners. They wouldn't talk. He kicked and shoved them while haranguing them with taunts and threats. They still wouldn't talk. Frustrated and frothing at the mouth, he whipped and lashed them with a stick until he dropped to the ground with exhaustion.

Chuck was awed at the way the man loathed his fellow countrymen and was glad he didn't have to be as cruel. *My job*, thought Chuck, *is to get a clean kill. It's more humane.*

"Let the professionals handle it," said the CO. He called for a helicopter to evacuate the prisoners to Da Nang.

With prisoners loaded, the helicopter rotors began to speed, lifting the skids to go. Suddenly, the interpreter ran up and leapt into the doorway.

Chuck and the other marines took the rare moment to rest, watching the helicopter rise straight up, getting smaller and smaller. As it lined up for Da Nang, a man came flying out the door backward, screaming in horror.

"That asshole interpreter threw the little bastard out," Chuck said to anyone who was listening. "They wouldn't talk, so he threw one of them out. I bet the other two are singing now."

The man somersaulted; the white rag blew off his eyes while his legs flailed as if he was running up a staircase. He spiraled and whirled toward the earth.

He hit the red dirt close enough for Chuck to hear the grinding splat and the air explode from his lungs.

Oh Lord, Chuck thought. The white rag came fluttering down, landing near the body.

Chuck slung his rifle and walked the few feet to the corpse. Chuck had seen a lot of dead bodies—shot up and bloody mostly. But this man's body wasn't punctured or bloody. His broken innards were held together inside the skin like a bag of potatoes. His bloodshot eyes were still looking at the ground rushing up at him.

"The party's over, assholes," said the CO. "Move out."

The marines paraded by Chuck and the body as if it were a viewing at the morgue. The last marine in line, walking close, stopped and looked solemnly at the body as if wondering what he, himself, would look like dead, then walked on following the column to the next piece of hell.

# 20

# WHEN PIGS FLY

**S**hortly after dawn one morning, Chuck and his spotter, Bill, were in a hide three hundred yards from a recently bombed-out Viet Cong–occupied village, observing in case Viet Cong returned. According to the plan, a helicopter was to pick them up at 4 p.m.

After hours of the team's hushed concentration, glassing the village and ignoring the calls of nature, a potbelly pig came snorting through the burnt-out village talking to himself, rooting through the debris for a morning meal. The sight of that homeless porker activated Chuck's sense of taste and smell. The thought of bacon and pork chops was maddening. Living on C-Rations month after month can drive a man berserk.

Bill whispered, "We're gonna kill it, aren't we, Chuck?"

"That's what I'm thinking. We'll wait until we hear the chopper coming, shoot it, stick it, and quick carry it to the LZ." Chuck knew the pilot would be in a hurry because helicopters attract attention. He'd want to stop, load, and go like hell.

"What if the pig leaves before our extraction?"

"If it looks like he's pulling out, I'll shoot him where he stands and we'll deal with it."

The pig had eaten breakfast and was looking for lunch when Chuck heard the *whap-whap-whap* of the helicopter. Chuck whacked the pig with a clean shot to the head. The boar hunters leapt from their hide on a haul-ass run for the dead pig. Chuck slit his throat with the Ka-Bar and gutted it in seconds. They each grabbed a hind leg and dragged the bloody pig to the idling helicopter.

They were met at the door by the crew chief wearing a helmet, a headset, and a frown. Pointing at the bloody carcass, he hollered, "You ain't putting that thing in my bird!"

"We ain't leaving here without it!" Chuck hollered back. He and Bill lifted the pig, two legs apiece.

"I guess you're walking!" hollered the chief, then

yelled through his mic to the pilot, "These idiots want to put a bloody pig in my helicopter!"

Chuck couldn't hear the other end of the conversation, but the pissed-off look on the crew chief's face indicated the pilot was antsy to load and leave.

The crew chief turned toward the pilot to argue. Chuck and Bill swung the pig through the door onto the shiny aluminum floor. Then they threw in their own crusty bodies. The pilot jammed the throttle, lifting the bird, as the crew chief pissed and pouted about the mess he'd have to clean up.

With the pig over Chuck's shoulder, he and Bill entered the base like Robin Hood and Little John returning to their Merry Men.

The troops debated how to cook the pig. "Back in Arkansas we put 'em on a spit." "How 'bout shish kebab?" and on and on until Fofo took over. "We're gonna cook this pig in the ground! You asshole marines dig me a hole, chop me up some wooden pallets, and round me up some banana leaves."

Chuck and Bill relaxed in the shade watching the work. While the marines got a rip-roaring fire going in the hole, Fofo skinned the beast with his Ka-Bar, then wrapped the carcass in banana leaves.

When the fire had died down enough to put the pig in, it was already 5:30. Fofo laid the wrapped pig on the coals, then, using his entrenching tool, covered it with dirt.

"How long we gonna have to wait?" Chuck yelled from the shade.

"Well," said Fofo, "this pig here weighs about eighty pounds, so it's gonna take five and a half hours."

A groan came up from the crowd.

"Dinner will be served at eleven p.m.," said Fofo.

Disappointed, Chuck, Bill, and the grunts departed for the mess hall with Fofo.

After chow, Chuck went with Fofo to monitor the cooking—staring at the mound of dirt.

About dark, the marines began to show up. Worried his timing might have been off, Fofo began to pace, licking his lips with his giant pink tongue until finally, at 11 p.m., he announced, "It's done!"

With the entrenching tool, he uncovered the pig. The aroma was intoxicating to the men who only had memories of such a smell. Four marines used their entrenching tools to steady the pig out of the hole and laid it on top of an artillery shell box.

One hundred men lined up.

With the Ka-Bar, Fofo sliced off a chunk of the steaming meat and dropped it into his upturned mouth. Smiling with his big white teeth, he called out, "Medium well!"

As Fofo cut the meat off the bones, Chuck proudly handed a piping-hot hunk to each man as they stepped by, thanking him. One of them said it's not often a grunt gets a gourmet meal this side of hell.

## 21

## "I'M SHOT UP"

**C**huck and his spotter, Dave, were assigned to Delta 1/5 during a large operation known as Meade River. The company was to find and engage a known Viet Cong and NVA stronghold in Dodge City in the area known as the "Mud Flats," over thirty square miles of rice paddies and tree lines.

Wearing full pack, Chuck was fourth in line, following Dave in a single line of sixty men, spaced ten yards apart. Chuck heard distant gunfire ahead. The radio crackled behind him. The column stopped. Chuck turned to see the CO take over the radio, then tell the man behind him, "Pass this back. We got marines in a hell of a jam. Let's move!"

Delta 1/5 pushed hard, humping across rice paddies.

The point man reached the cover of a tree line. Dave was about twenty yards out, and Chuck was ten yards behind him, trotting next to a six-inch-high dike.

AK-47 fire erupted to the left, about two hundred yards up the tree line. Dave and the marine ahead of him plunged into the cover of the tree line. Bullets splashed around Chuck, and he dropped on his stomach, facedown in the mud behind the little dike, his rifle clutched in his outstretched hands. Marines screamed in terror and pain. Chuck hugged the mud, but his backpack was exposed like a camel's hump. Desperate to get to cover, he began inching for the tree line.

His left shoulder was hit like from a baseball bat. But it didn't hurt. He stopped moving, wondering if he'd been shot. He'd never been shot. He moved ahead, just to be hit again. It still didn't hurt. Chuck stayed still, worrying he was dead meat, thinking, *I gotta get out of here.*

Staying low like a worm he moved again and was hit again. *Just like the point man. I'm living the hell he went through. But still no pain. Maybe I'm already dead. Maybe in heaven already? Or is this hell?* His mind rushed from one scenario to the next until his instinct to survive took over again. Attempting a fast belly crawl, he took another hit, stopping him just a few feet from the tree line. Still no pain, but he felt warm liquid running down his sides. *Blood,* Chuck thought, *and lots of it. I'm bleeding out. How's Mom gonna feel when she gets the telegram? I should have been a better boy.*

Jets came screaming in, rockets pulverizing the enemy position, shaking the mud under him. Thank God! With the enemy distracted, Chuck lunged on his belly the last feet. Dave pulled him to safety, rolled him into the brush, and got back to business.

Chuck was relieved to be with Dave. Now he could bleed to death in peace.

Looking up through flowering treetops at gentle fluffy clouds floating by, he crossed his hands like he was a body in a casket. He felt blood oozing between his fingers. He looked down. It wasn't blood. It was a yellowish syrup.

Then he remembered. That morning he'd loaded his backpack with canned peaches.

# 22

# THE ONE WHO GOT AWAY

**A**fter three months in-country, marines were up for R & R. Chuck picked Bangkok, Thailand. Bangkok had been quiet until the Vietnam War, when GIs began storming the place, so some businesses changed to hothouses of drink, drugs, and whores.

As was required by the Marine Corps, before Chuck could depart he had to leave his rifle at the armorer's tent. "Don't be messing with this," Chuck told the armorer. "I shoot it every day and it's right on."

"I'll be the judge of that," said the armorer as he grabbed the weapon.

Chuck left for Bangkok worrying about his rifle and what the man would do to it.

He and a buddy spent five days and nights in the company of two young prostitutes. Chuck was giddy and tired when he returned to An Hoa.

First off, he went straight to the armorer's tent to get his rifle. It was a cold reunion. Smirking, the armorer dropped the rifle on the counter. His eyes were hooded like he was hiding something—like he was somehow getting in the last lick. Figuring the little fucker had changed things around, Chuck planned to sight it in as soon as he got to Delta Company.

The armorer grunted a "fuck you" and turned back to his workbench.

Relieved to have his gun back, Chuck pulled out his rag and wiped down the gun right there on the counter.

On the chopper going out to Delta Company, he realized he'd missed his marines. It would be great to see them again. But first he would have to sight in his gun.

Just as the helicopter idled down for the unload, Chuck heard gunfire; a battle was taking place about a mile off to the west. He was told that Bravo Company was engaging the enemy, but Delta wouldn't be called to assist, so Chuck moved to the edge of the perimeter to sight in his rifle.

He was sitting on a rock loading the rifle when he spotted a farmer crossing a rice paddy about three hundred yards out. Something about the guy got Chuck's attention. He wasn't looking at the crop of rice like a farmer would. He moved along steady— maybe away from the battle. So Chuck got interested. The guy was old for a Viet Cong—maybe forty, bake faced, strange dark eyes Chuck could see even at that distance. The man was dragging something with a rope deep in the rice where it couldn't be seen. He looked up and saw Chuck, his eyes widened, he turned, and walked directly away. He came to a dike. As he stepped over it, Chuck saw the rifle—the man was going down. Chuck squeezed off a shot. The man turned toward Chuck with dark, god-awful eyes. Then he turned and ran with Chuck blazing away, shooting high right, low right, high left, and low left—missing every time.

The next time Chuck was at An Hoa, he had a talk with the armorer. "What the hell did you do to my rifle? I told you not to mess with it."

"What ya mean? I adjust all the rifles. They come here in bad shape and I fix 'em."

"Mine didn't need fixing. I take good care of it. Now, because of your handiwork, I let a VC go. Who knows how many marines he'll kill."

"I can't help it if you can't shoot straight."

Chuck was about to retaliate when he noticed a stack of boxes in the shadows at the back of the tent, not painted green. Five cases of Pabst Blue Ribbon beer.

Early in the first tour. Still a grunt, guarding the bridge at Phu Bai.

With other snipers at An Hoi.

*All these photos are from Chuck Mawhinney's private collection.*

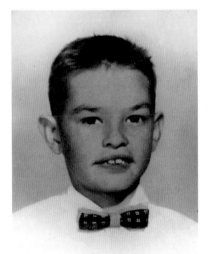

Chuck in second grade.

Circle track racing senior year high school.

Chuck (called Charlie at the time) in high school.

Chuck with his airplane in high school.

First furlough at
Bangkok.

Chuck (left) hunting with George.

Second tour. On the trail.

Second tour at An Hoi with a spotter.

A very young-looking Chuck on his first tour as sniper.

Relaxing next to a pack mule in An Hoi.

Receiving a field promotion from generals
at Liberty Bridge combat base.

Chuck's second tour at An Hoi.

Chuck hanging from a net with a recon outfit bound for Laos.

Village children friends of Chuck.
Note the one on the left, who is enjoying a cigarette.

Liberty Bridge, Song River, near the Liberty Bridge combat
base. Four miles to the right on the river is where Chuck
stopped a battalion of NVA.

Chuck catches an armed Viet Cong in the cross hairs.
He snapped this picture and then dispatched the man.

Chuck with his spotter, observing enemy activity.

Ho Chi Minh trail photographed by Chuck.

Late second tour - Chuck (left) on the trail with his spotter.

Chuck holding up Sugar Bear at An Hoi.

**CHARLEY MAWHINNEY**

Lance Corporal Charles B. Mawhinney, son of Mr. and Mrs. Charles P. Mawhinney of 230 South E. Street Lakeview, will complete his tour of duty in Vietnam on July 13, and will return to the United States at that time.

Corporal Mawhinney has served as a sniper with the 5th Marine Regiment while in Vietnam. He has been awarded the Purple Heart and cluster for being wounded on two occasions and has received the Navy Commendation Medal. He has also been recommended for the Bronze Star and Silver Star Medals.

The young Marine expects to return to Lakeview on July 20 to begin a 20-day leave, at the end of which time he will be reassigned by the U. S. Marine Corps for further duty.

A Lakeview newspaper's article about Chuck getting wounded near the end of his first tour.

Chuck (center) with fellow snipers and spotters
in front of the sniper tent at An Hoi.

Chuck used this M-14 with the night scope to stop the NVA
battalion from crossing the Thu Bon River.

Enemy prisoners caught escaping
a local village.

Semper Fi.
The creed
of a Marine.

## Ask Me What I Was

I'll reply with what I've done.
Those things others would not do, I did:
Those rivers others would not swim, I swam:
Those hills others would not climb, I conquered;
Those bridges others would not cross, I crossed;
I have celebrated, I have mourned.
I have smiled and I have frowned.
I have seen death and felt its warm breath.
It did not faze me,
For I was different, I was a warrior.
You ask me what I was? It was my destiny.
Until my last breath,
To be a United States Marine,
And my spirit shall live forever.

**Semper Fidelis**
**For I was, am and shall forever**
**be a**
**"United States Marine"**

Hunting during his USFS career.

Sniper reunion.
Chuck (third from right) standing between Mark and Sugar Bear.

Nobody had beer like that around An Hoa. Chuck figured the armorer was stealing it—probably from the grunts who earned it. Chuck pulled his eyes away. He left the tent, his mouth watering. He would not forget that beer.

## 23

# THE MAPMAKER

**S**till agonizing over the stolen Pabst in the armorer's tent, Chuck was standing with Bill, observing a large rice paddy from the edge of the company's perimeter. It was close to Liberty Bridge—maybe a mile from where the dark-eyed man had gotten away.

A man stepped into Chuck's rifle scope, about six hundred yards out, walking from a brush line toward the middle of the paddy where the rice was knee high.

"What we got here?" said Chuck.

"Looks like a farmer to me," said Bill, looking through his field glasses. "He's wearing the right attire."

"Since when is a straw hat and pajamas attire?"

"Maybe his wife won't dress him."

"He doesn't seem to be doing much farming," Chuck said, getting suspicious. "He's mostly interested in our perimeter."

"Yeah, he keeps looking over here. He's not picking us out. But he's carrying a rope."

Interested, Chuck slid down into prone position, readying for a long shot, but not in a hurry. The man was in the middle of the paddy and wasn't going anywhere soon. So Chuck didn't have to rush to judgment about whether the man would live or die. "I'll bet you that rope's tied to a gun. I'd bet a case of beer on it if I had one."

Kneeling now, Bill said, "I'm done betting with you, Chuck. You always win."

"Tell that to Mark the next time I play Back Alley Bridge with him. I can't beat the guy."

The man stepped on a dike showing a rifle. Just like the other episode.

"He's got a gun," Bill whispered.

Chuck's bolt gun had five-hundred-meter DOPE on it—in that distance the bullet would drop twenty-six inches. Chuck put the reticle on the man's head, figuring the bullet would hit him center mass, in the chest. Ready to pull the trigger, he smelled cigarette smoke and heard grunts talking behind him.

Bill laughed. "Hey, we got an audience."

"This is the first time for that," Chuck said. "I better

not miss." Between breaths, he began to squeeze the trigger. He heard the click of a camera.

He let out his breath, put down the rifle, and looked up at a grinning Bill. "What the hell?"

Bill shrugged. The grunts laughed.

Chuck kept his eye on the target, listening for the mood to change. When the grunts got quiet, he raised his rifle—the man dropped like a stone.

The grunts cheered. A five-man fire team, including an officer, walked the six hundred yards to the corpse, searched the body, and returned with the gun and a sling made of nylon parachute rope, and a folded piece of paper.

"You hit him center mass, Chuck," said the officer, pulling his pen. "Give me your kill sheet." While signing it, he said, "He didn't know what hit him." He handed Chuck a folded piece of paper that looked to Chuck like a homemade map. "He's been drawing a layout of our company, showing where the guns and ammo are. He was a bad boy. You did good, Chuck."

## 24

# BEER THIRTY

**C**huck and his spotter Bill were due to return for their monthly three-day debriefing back at An Hoa. Chuck could either wait a day for a helicopter to fly them to An Hoa, or jump on a helicopter right then, get dropped three miles from the base, and walk in. The lure of a shower and real food got the best of him. So from the helicopter's drop-off point, he and Bill, with full packs in horrendous heat, humped the distance, dreaming of the clean running water and soap they hadn't felt in a month.

After checking in at the gate, they plodded exhausted through dusty alleys for the snipers' tent, where they'd leave their gear then head to the showers. Between them and the tent were the showers, open-top and backed by a sandbagged bunker. Nearing the shower entrance, Chuck smelled fresh soap and heard Mark Limpic bitching to himself about not having warm water. They met him as he was about to go in, wearing shorts with a towel wrapped around his neck.

"Hi Chuck," he said, nodding to Bill. "Nice to see you back. I'm readying to take another cold-water shower. You'd think the Corps would have a little respect for us living out here in the wild."

"Yeah," Chuck said, sweating in his own filth. "All I been thinking about out there for the last month is how bad you got it here."

"That's nice." Mark stepped around the corner into the showers.

Chuck grinned, handed his rifle to Bill, dropped his pack in the dust, and said, "Hell, he wants a warm shower. I'll give him one." He made a running jump to the top of the bunker overlooking Mark, who was soaping under the cold water. Chuck dropped his pants, pulled out his manhood for the whole world to see, and with full flow, shot a stream of warmth into the side of his superior's neck.

Eyes closed, Mark turned his smiling face into the balmy fluid. He squinched his nose, looked up, and gave out a tortured holler. He ran from the showers soaped and naked. "You son of a bitch!" he yelled up at Chuck, who was bent over laughing.

Sobering, Chuck pulled up his pants, wondering what the outcome would be. Would he be court-martialed? He looked at the naked man standing in the dust, soaped and furious.

Mark's face went blank, then broke out in a big smile, then he laughed. Bill laughed. Mark looked around at the curious bystanders, then hurried back into the showers.

Grateful that Mark could take a joke, Chuck took his gun back from Bill and they trudged to the snipers' tent and civilization.

⊕

At about 1 a.m. the second night, Chuck was awakened by a loud card game in the smoke-filled tent. His squad leader Mark Limpic and some other snipers were playing Back Alley Bridge on an ammunition crate under a light bulb. Chuck couldn't get back to sleep, so he decided to join in.

"Sure would be nice to have some beer," Mark said. "Nobody plays cards without beer."

"I know where we can get some Pabst," Chuck said. "It's stashed about a dozen doors down the alley."

Suddenly a rocket screamed overhead. The tent went dark; the emergency siren blared, meaning *run for the bunkers!*

Chuck and Mark were the last to leave, almost crashing into a M274 Mule parked outside the door flap, giving Chuck an idea. "Let's go for a ride!" Chuck yelled as he jumped on the little truck and fired up the motor.

"Are you out of your mind?" Mark hollered over the sounds of rockets and mortars coming in and An Hoa artillery shooting back. "There's a war going on, if you haven't noticed!"

"Get on!" Chuck yelled. "It's beer thirty!"

"We're going to risk our lives for beer?" Mark leapt on the Mule.

Chuck stuck his foot into the carburetor and tore down the deserted alley as rockets whistled and mortars pounded around them. "Gimme your Ka-Bar! We don't have a key!"

Mark handed over the knife.

Chuck stopped behind the armorer's tent. Leaving the motor running, he cut a five-foot-long slit, vertical like gutting a moose. He entered and blindly groped around in the dark, bumping here and there until he laid his hands on a case of beer about shoulder high. Eureka! He handed the first one through the slit as a rocket flashed, lighting up Mark's face. He looked terrified. "Load this!" Chuck hollered.

"Okay! Now let's go!"

"Whoa! There's more!"

Chuck passed Mark three more cases then slammed

his ass down on the Mule, horseshoed around, and throttled for home through explosions, smoke, and the smell of burning sulfur.

"Did you get all of it?!" yelled Mark.

"There's one more!"

"Why didn't we take it?!"

"You can't take a guy's last beer! It's the rule!"

They rushed the beer into the snipers' tent, then ran the few feet to a trench and dove in.

The rockets quit. The lights came on.

The monster rat didn't get a minute's sleep that night with his roomies gurgling and burping themselves drunk on warm beer.

# 25

# ROK ADVENTURE

The Republic of South Korea sent many soldiers to fight in Vietnam, and one day Chuck was asked to help an ROK marine unit nearby. He would never know the exact reason for the summons or why he was sent without his spotter. But evidently they needed the services of the long gun.

Chuck arrived at the ROK unit by helicopter. Right off he went looking for the man in charge. He couldn't understand a word the ROK grunts said, and they couldn't understand him. Finally, he found a man who spoke some English and seemed to be in charge.

Despite the mystery of what in hell he was there

for, Chuck went out each day on patrols with the ROK marines. They were ornery little fellas who would walk behind him and pepper his back and legs with sticks when he wasn't looking. It was obvious they had no respect for him.

Another thing that bothered Chuck when on patrol was that they didn't set up for the night. Instead of creating a perimeter, they dropped wherever—maybe in a hut of an abandoned village or they'd just curl up along a trail, leaving Chuck wide-eyed and sleepless. If a sound woke the Koreans, they'd grab their weapons and run out into the dark to investigate. If an enemy was caught alive they just beat him to death and went back to bed.

To make Chuck's job even more difficult, the leadership of the ROK unit seemed to change daily—like whoever was the toughest SOB that day was king.

Chuck considered the ROK some badass dudes and was glad they were on his side.

One day Chuck was in the middle of the column on patrol with them when the ROKs ahead of him hunkered down in some tall grass. Curious, Chuck moved ahead to where the ROKs were pointing to NVA who were lingering out in a rice paddy at least six hundred yards away. The ROK marines pointed around and chattered, like they were going to try to sneak up on the NVA.

Chuck lay down among them and rested his rifle barrel on the dike. From the corner of his eye, he saw them wag their heads in disbelief: no one could kill a man at that distance. Chuck aimed and fired; an NVA went down. With two more shots he'd killed two more. By then the other NVA had scattered into a tree line, saving themselves.

The ROK marines were wide-eyed. They grinned and patted Chuck with respect, obviously proud of him. From then on, they showed him off, so any passersby would assume that Chuck was part of their company.

And Chuck was happy he'd survived another two weeks of duty and the ROK marines.

## 26

# THE GREASE GUN

**C**huck and Bill were called out to a Combined Action Platoon (CAP). CAP was a marine counterinsurgency program to help win the hearts and minds of the residents. Each unit consisted of a dozen or so soldiers who lived within villages, teaching the inhabitants basic first aid, clean water, and food preservation.

Upon arriving at the village by helicopter, Chuck and Bill checked in with the CO. Chuck eyed the short-barreled machine gun hanging from the CO's belt.

"What can we do for you, sir?" Chuck asked.

"We got an enemy sniper harassing us. Early every morning he shoots at us a few times, and then after we turn in, the same thing. He's getting on our nerves. Can you deal with it?"

"Don't worry," said Chuck. "We'll get the shooter soon as we find out where he's shooting from. That's quite a gun you got there. What is it?"

"It's a grease gun," said the CO. "Forty-five caliber, full auto."

"I could use one of them. This long gun isn't much good up close, and my pistol is a slow shooter. Where'd you get it?" he asked, pointing at the grease gun.

He grinned. "I got lucky. Won it in a poker game."

Chuck liked the guy.

That evening, Chuck and Bill were in a bunker playing cards, waiting for the expected shot. The shot rang out; Chuck sprang through the doorway in time to hear the second round and pinpoint the direction from where it had come.

Before daylight, Chuck and Bill set a course for the shooter, then, with Chuck a short distance behind Bill, they left on a trail. In the blackness they crossed rice paddies and groped through tree lines, sniper hunting sniper.

At daybreak, Chuck was surprised when the morning mist revealed the silhouette of a small group of huts close up.

Suddenly Bill raised his M14 and fired ahead at a target Chuck couldn't see.

"Hit," said Bill.

*Hey*, Chuck thought, *I'm the shooter here.*

They approached the body. They found an older man lying on his back, dead with a cold rifle clutched in his hands. Like the man, the gun was old—maybe World War II era—and held together with concertina wire.

"The man musta wanted to die," said Bill.

"How's that?"

"He stepped out from the tree line and threw his gun up like he was gonna shoot me. He never had a chance."

Chuck figured the old man was their sniper. They left the body where it lay and, with Bill carrying the old gun over his shoulder, hiked back to the unit happy and ever vigilant.

Chuck with a grin offered up the good news to the CO, handing over the old rifle. "Thanks to Bill, your sniper troubles are over."

"I appreciate that." The CO unhooked the grease gun from his belt and handed it to Chuck. "Here. You need this way more than I do."

Chuck thought about giving Bill the grease gun—he'd earned it. But, remembering the episode with Albury, he decided he'd better take the gun when he had the chance.

# 27

# FIRST FURLOUGH HOME

Chuck's first tour was over. He'd survived thirteen months in one of the most dangerous areas in Vietnam. And as a sniper, he was averaging six kills a week. Now it was time for his first leave, to go home and reenter a life he could hardly remember. The thought of leaving his buddies behind and unprotected bothered him.

Chuck had a choice; he could either simply go home on a thirty-day furlough then be reassigned duty somewhere besides Vietnam, or he could re-up now for a second tour, go home for thirty days, then return to his old outfit for another six months.

He'd learned so much in thirteen months and knew

the country very well—the terrain and the enemy's mind and how it reacted. His job wasn't over yet. He re-upped.

He would take the same route as before but in reverse: Da Nang to Okinawa to Oakland, and then he would change planes for Klamath Falls.

Chuck boarded the plane for home wearing fresh fatigues and sporting a new military haircut. He flew with other jovial marines going to the states on furlough or for good.

He first stepped on US soil in Oakland, California. Most of the other marines were met by wives, girlfriends, or parents. Alone, Chuck crowded through the mass reunion to look for the gate to Klamath Falls and was accosted by a horde of screaming war protesters—flower-powered hippies giving him the finger and cursing him. "Village burner!" yelled a female, with hate-filled eyes behind rose-colored glasses. "Baby killer," hissed a bearded, tie-dyed stoner. Reeking with patchouli oil and marijuana, the protesters crowded Chuck as he strode with his head high down the concourse.

Normal people looked away in shame—was it shame on him or shame on themselves for not supporting him?

When Chuck got to the gate for Klamath Falls, and

its passengers of farmers, loggers, and mill workers, the protesters lost interest and returned to the gates coming from Vietnam so they could terrorize the next soldier boy coming home.

Back in Lakeview, Mom and Dad hadn't changed, only maybe the wrinkles were a little deeper and their hair a little grayer, from worry, Chuck supposed. It was nice to see them. Mom admired his haircut and Dad shook his hand with respect in his eyes. Chuck had missed them more than he'd thought.

"So, Dennis is gone," Chuck said, "what about my other friends? Anyone still around or are most gone off to the service?"

"I see some of your classmates downtown now and then," Mom said. "They don't say much."

"I think I'll run down and see what's happening," Chuck said. "Can I borrow the pickup, Dad?"

Dad smiled. "Keys are in it."

First thing, Chuck went to his room and changed into his civvies. His jeans felt strange. So did driving; he hadn't been behind the wheel in a year.

Chuck pulled into the A&W. Suzie was still carhopping.

"Hi Suzie, I'll have a root beer."

"Where you been, Charley?"

"Gone—way gone. Where is everyone?"

"Pretty much working now," she said. "Come night

they'll be drinking. Working and drinking—that's pretty much it nowadays."

"So where do they do the drinking?"

"Up at Drews Reservoir lately," she said. "Go up there tonight. You'll find some old friends."

"What time?"

"About dark."

Driving Dad's pickup, Chuck got to Drews Reservoir just before dark. The mountain lake where he and his family had camped when he was a kid looked just as Chuck remembered—blue water surrounded by giant trees and ducks flying and fish jumping. How could it be so peaceful here? There's no misery of bombs and booby traps. It's like there is no war.

No people at the lake, except for on the opposite bank, where a couple cars were parked and a campfire burned near the water. *Bet that's them.* Chuck drove the gravel road that circled the lake. Getting close, he saw kids standing around the fire on the rocky shore. Some he recognized but none were friends. He pulled up and got out.

"Hi Charley," said a boy he knew from school. "Have a beer with us."

"Thanks," Chuck said, joining the circle around the fire.

The boy pulled a can from the cooler and handed it to him. "So what's it like over there in Nam anyway?"

Chuck took a long swig from the can. "Hot."

The kids laughed, then the boy started off about his new job at the sawmill.

Chuck could tell he didn't want to know what it was like in Nam. "I'll drink to that," he said to no one and took another swallow.

"What?" asked an unfamiliar ponytailed girl, kicking at the fire.

"Nothing," said Chuck. She wouldn't understand. *Nobody here understands. How could they? I'm the one who's been killing and living like a wild animal.*

Darkness fell. Chuck heard night sounds coming from the forest surrounding the lake, and his senses picked up: crickets and frogs and an owl, not a lot different from night sounds he'd heard in Vietnam.

More beers and more logs on the fire. The flames snapped and popped and the kids laughed at each other's faces lit up by the blaze.

*They haven't changed,* Chuck thought. *They're still the same kids I left a year ago. I'm out of place here.*

Fueled by the alcohol, the kids got singing and shouting and laughing. The fire got bigger, sending sparks into the sky. The night sounds stopped. Chuck got jittery. He tried to assure himself that they were safe, but found himself doing a perimeter check. Coming back to the fire, he saw the kids laughing at him. Chuck didn't laugh. Then nobody was laughing. Nobody looked at Chuck. The girl kicked at the fire again.

"I'll be going now," he said to no one in particular.

Nobody said goodbye.

Driving off the mountain, rejected, it jolted Chuck that he was no longer one of the bunch. *Hell—I used to lead those punks around.* He longed for his real friends back in Vietnam.

In town, Chuck recognized a car parked in front of the local tavern. It belonged to Dave, a mechanic Chuck knew from the Ford garage.

A little bell tinkled when he opened the tavern door. Everyone looked at Chuck. Dave smiled. "Charley, you're home! Come over here to the bar. I'm buying you a beer."

Chuck needed that smile more than a beer, but he wasn't going to turn one down. He shook Dave's hand and crawled up on the barstool. He felt a small pang of guilt since it would be two more years before he could legally drink in a tavern. He placed his hands down on the long wooden bar weathered by cigarette burns and scarred by years of the hardened elbows of working men and women. He looked into the large mirror of the back bar and saw a man looking back. He'd changed in thirteen months. His guilt evaporated in an instant. He was a man now.

The bartender appeared from the back room. He was a big guy wearing an apron and wielding a bar rag. "What'll it be?" he asked Chuck.

"Make it a Hamm's," Chuck said. "A stubby, just like Dave here's drinking."

The bartender pulled the bottle from the cooler and set it down in front of Chuck. Then looking up, stared at him. "How old are you, boy?"

"Old enough." Chuck stared back.

"Show me," the bartender said.

"Give him the beer," said Dave. "He's just come home from war. If he's old enough to fight for you he's old enough for a beer."

"I ain't serving him without seeing his ID."

Chuck knew he couldn't fight the law. That's why he'd left Lakeview. Without taking his eyes off the bartender, he rose from the barstool and slid the Hamm's over in front of Dave. "Thanks anyway, Dave."

Chuck couldn't wait to get back to his real friends.

# 28

# THE STOLEN GREASE GUN

**C**huck happily arrived back in Vietnam to a robust re-union with his marines. Soon it was back to work for Chuck.

*Damn. Another swinging dick is sporting corporal chevrons,* Chuck thought when another peer got pro-moted. Day after day someone would come back from An Hoa shouldering E-4 stripes. They'd be grinning and bragging. It was eating on Chuck pretty good, and of course everyone was having fun with it at his ex-pense. "Where's *your* chevrons, Mawhinney?"

"Hell, I don't know." He wondered why he was still

an E-3, when he hadn't been in any trouble and was near a hundred kills.

On the last day in May, Chuck was assigned to Delta 1/5, who at the time were out in Arizona Territory. He heard the *whap, whap* of a distant helicopter coming in. It could mean mail, food, ammo, or a familiar face. The bird landed. From across the perimeter, Chuck saw Mark Limpic step down on the dirt, and wondered what his squad leader was doing all the way out there. *Am I finally going to An Hoa for promotion?*

Chuck and Carter hurried to meet Mark, who said, "You guys are flying with me to Liberty Bridge tomorrow."

*Damn.* "Not An Hoa?"

"Nope. Where's the CO?"

Chuck pointed him out and Mark left.

"Jeez, Chuck," Carter said. "What kind of crusade are we going on now?"

"Maybe we're going after Ho Chi Minh himself."

"Oh God, not him!"

Later, Chuck and Carter were outside their tent when Mark showed up flashing a pair of shiny, hand-powered hair clippers and told Chuck, "We've got to spruce you up a bit."

The cold chrome tool looked painful, like something a surgeon would use. Chuck shuddered. "Why would we wanna do that?"

"You need a haircut."

Carter said, "Well, I don't need one."

"Right," said Mark. "You're okay."

Chuck sat on a box, flinching, while Carter watched and Mark, not a barber, nicked and gouged hair from his scalp.

Running his fingers through what was left, Chuck said, "Shit, Mark! I feel like I've been mowed with a dull lawn mower."

"You two have your gear ready in the morning," said Mark. "We're leaving after chow."

Next morning, the three piled into a helicopter and flew to Liberty Bridge, for why, no one was saying. But Chuck looked forward to better food and honest-to-goodness showers.

They stepped from the helicopter. Chuck and Carter followed Mark into a gauntlet of curious marines, clean-shaven and smelling of Ivory soap, gaping at Chuck's sniper rifle and into his eyes.

Bewildered, Chuck muttered to Carter, "They've never looked at me like this before."

"Maybe they heard about the St. Valentine's Day massacre."

"That got around fast."

Chuck and Carter followed Mark into the compound, up one of the red dirt streets lined with gawkers in front of permanent tents.

At the visitors' tent, Mark told Carter, "Stay here and keep an eye on the gear. Chuck will be back to get you after a while." Then he led the way to what turned out to be the showers.

During a scrub from heaven, Chuck was still wondering why the marines were acting the way they were. In clean fatigues, a hat, and shiny new boots that were too small for him, he ignored the pain in his feet as he followed Mark to the dirt formation grounds, where the bleachers were filled with marines, excited like they were ready to watch a football game.

Chuck eyed five men standing in the center of the formation grounds, starched and grouped, talking with the CO like they were planning an invasion. Chuck was surprised to see four of them dripping with brass. Nervous, he wondered, *Could all this be for me?*

Mark led Chuck out to them. Three generals and a lieutenant colonel turned and acknowledged them through aviation sunglasses. Chuck and Mark saluted and the officers introduced themselves.

Chuck then saw metal chevrons sparkling in Lt. General Nickerson's hand.

Chuck was blown away. It was unheard of to have generals field-promote a lance corporal, and here were three of them.

The CO shouted for attention—the bleachers turned quiet and Chuck could hear his own watch ticking. The CO read the report about Chuck's many accomplishments as a sniper. Lt. General Nickerson stuck the pins into Chuck's shirt and then punched them with his fist hard, through the cotton and into Chuck's hide, drawing blood.

There was applause from the bleachers as the generals congratulated him, impressing Chuck with their serious respectfulness.

"If you ever need some help from us," said Lt. General Nickerson, "don't hesitate to come find us. Goodbye and good luck."

The officers turned and strode off to their bunker, signaling the party was over.

Chuck turned to a grinning Mark. They shook hands, then Mark was off to the LZ for a flight back to An Hoa.

Chuck returned to Carter, who was still standing next to the gear—but now with a worried look on his face.

"What's wrong?" asked Chuck.

"A corporal came and took your grease gun."

"*What?* Why didn't you tell him to go to hell?"

"He told me the sergeant major sent him for it— said you weren't supposed to have it. They had me outranked."

"Oh yeah?" Chuck was pissed. "I'm gonna talk to the generals about this."

Ready to knock on the door of the officers' bunker, Chuck thought, *It seems a little soon to use the favor. But oh well.*

He knocked on the door with purpose.

It swung open to a corporal with protective eyes. Behind him, Lt. General Nickerson was sitting with the others at a table under a light bulb in the smoke-filled bunker.

Chuck said, "I would like to speak with General Nickerson."

The general rose. "What can I do for you, sniper?"

Hat in hand, Chuck recounted the story of the stolen grease gun.

"Where did this theft take place?"

"At the visitors' tent."

"I know where that is. You need that gun?"

"Yessir."

"Well," the general said. "We'll take care of it. Go back to the tent and wait for us."

"Thank you, sir!"

Impressed with himself for asking, Chuck started back to his tent, wondering how the sergeant major was going to like his encounter with General Nickerson.

Carter was still standing there, looking anxious. "What did the generals say?"

"They went to get the gun back."

Carter said, "I'd like to be there to see Mister Sergeant Major's face when he meets the generals."

Soon Chuck spotted the generals approaching from the direction of the cook shack, Lt. General Nickerson out in front carrying the grease gun. It reminded

Chuck of the famous picture of Douglas MacArthur stepping onto the beach in the Philippines.

Chuck and Carter saluted.

"Nice weapon you got here, Mawhinney." General Nickerson smiled. "It's made the rounds today. After it left your spotter here, it was handed off to the sergeant major and then sold to the cook." He placed it in Chuck's hands with a wink.

The officers' names were: Lt. General Henry Buse Jr., Commanding General of Fleet Marine Forces Pacific; Colonel Zaro, 5th Marines; Lt. Colonel William Riley Jr., Command Officer of 1st Battalion, 5th Marine Regiment; and Lt. General Herman Nickerson Jr., a medal-laden combat vet who had served in World War II and Korea.

# 29

# ON THE RANGE
# WITH JIM LAND

**C**huck was working with Captain Mike Wiley's Delta 1/5 when he got the call to report to Da Nang for rifle re-qualification, a routine order just for snipers that Chuck had done before. Normally he'd be overjoyed since it meant hanging out with snipers and shooting at paper targets.

But Delta 1/5 was about to join an operation close to the Laos border—a hot area—so would need Chuck more than ever. He'd been averaging several kills a week, so he knew he didn't need to re-qualify. The last thing he needed was to go shoot at targets while his fellow marines engaged in dangerous combat. Wiley tried to intervene but couldn't get the order canceled. So Chuck would be away in Da Nang for three days. How could it take three days to shoot up a target? He hadn't left yet but was already annoyed.

His first morning of re-qualifying, Chuck slouched in a folding chair in the last row of snipers, glaring at the front wall of the tent where a thousand-yard paper target hung as big as a tablecloth, its black rings centering a black bull's-eye the size of a dinner plate.

Standing beside it, the events instructor, Sergeant Al Whitby, was saying, "... and at a thousand yards, you'll each get five shots at a target just like this one, with a maximum of five minutes for each shot."

*Five minutes? Why would it take five minutes? I can do it in five seconds.*

Whitby continued, "You will notice this target has five holes near the bull's-eye. It shows the highest score on this range until now, and it happens to be me who shot it."

A murmur of admiration went through the snipers except for Chuck, who was thinking, *I can do better than that. Shit, the target isn't even shooting back.*

Out at the range, it was a perfect day for shooting, no wind on a crystal clear morning, but Chuck grumbled inside, waiting for his turn to shoot. The first group of four shooters had just assumed the prone position facing the targets. At a thousand yards—the distance of ten football fields—the bull's-eye was a mere speck.

"Fire at will!" called Whitby.

The men took their time with the first shot. Waiting for them to take their second, Chuck checked his watch and paced with a scowl, fuming under his breath, "Taking a long time to shoot." Time dragged on until finally the first group had shot up their ammo.

"Clear rifles," called Whitby, signaling the shooting was over.

The shooters stood up. Then Chuck and all the other snipers accompanied by Whitby piled onto Mules and, with their boots dangling in the red dust, putted the overloaded vehicles a thousand yards to investigate the targets. Everyone unloaded. Whitby collected the four targets and spread them on the Mule beds for scoring. Chuck was let down by the results. Most bullets had hit the targets somewhere but weren't grouped well and weren't near the bull's-eye.

Whitby rolled up the four targets and gave each shooter his. Then they all rattled back to the firing line, where Chuck's attitude worsened as he endured four more shooters taking their time.

He was about to implode with restlessness when he heard helicopter blades accelerate. A C-46 rose from an LZ near the gun range and swung west. About a mile out, it exploded in a ball of flame. Chuck heard the explosion as the flaming helicopter was crashing into trees. *Oh my God!*

He looked at the other snipers for their reaction—they were still staring at the targets. They might not have seen the disaster but they had to have heard it. It felt surreal, the way the shooters were so absorbed in their craft they were detached from death.

After another putt-putt ride to bring back the targets, it was finally Chuck's time to shoot. He dropped to prone position in row three and placed his rifle on the sandbags. All he had to do now was wait for Whitby's call.

Finally, "Fire at will!"

Chuck chambered the first round, aimed his rifle, and fired, sending the bullet and his pent-up frustration on their way. Then he quickly bolted in the next and let it go, too. He aimed and shot three more times in a matter of seconds.

Feeling better, he laid the warm rifle down.

"Clear rifles," ordered Whitby.

*Why? The others aren't done.* Baffled, Chuck stood up with the others.

Everyone was staring at him, slack-jawed.

Chuck stared back at them, *What did I do?*

Whitby stepped up close to Chuck, nose to nose, his breath smelling like turpentine. "You got a problem, asshole? No one shoots like that during qualifying. You makin' a mockery of the United States Marine Corps?"

"No sir, I mean yes sir! I mean I really need to be

with my outfit. They're about to be sent into some deep shit and they need me. Sir!"

Whitby turned back to the other shooters and nodded. They resumed the prone position. Focused on the shooters, Whitby called, "Fire at will!"

Chuck relaxed. He was relieved Whitby had moved on.

As the shooters slowly began popping off the rest of their rounds, Chuck noticed a jeep pull up with a captain riding shotgun. The captain disembarked and strode with confidence for the firing line. Chuck and the other spectators saluted him, but he waved off the salutes and became engrossed in the target shooting. Chuck was impressed by the captain's interest.

When the shooting was over, everyone loaded up on the Mules as before. To Chuck's surprise, the captain piled on one of the dirty little Mules for the dusty trip.

At the target site, Chuck stepped off the Mule and looked at target number three. All his shots were in the bull's-eye. *Goddamn, that's honest shooting. Even for me.*

Everyone stared at Chuck's target.

"Who shot number three?" asked the captain.

Everyone stared at Chuck, speechless with reverence.

"That would be me, sir," Chuck replied like he shot this way every day, which he did. "Lance Corporal Chuck Mawhinney, sir."

"Damn good, Corporal," said the captain. "Damn, damn good."

"Thank you, sir."

Whitby removed the target with respect and handed it to the captain like it was the Holy Grail. The captain spread the target on a Mule's bed and admired it for a time. Then to Chuck he said, "Come here, Corporal."

Curious now, Chuck smartly stepped up.

The captain took a pen from his pocket and said, "I'm going to sign this target, then I want you to sign it, as well as Sergeant Whitby." Then to Whitby, "I want you to hang this target in the classroom tent, for God and everyone to see."

The captain signed his name in the lower left corner: *Jim Land.*

Chuck stared at the signature in awe. He'd heard about Jim Land in sniper school, but never thought he'd get to meet him—let alone on a little rifle range in Vietnam. Jim Land was known as the father of the Marine Corps Scout Sniper program. A decorated marksman himself, he'd started the program in 1961. What Chuck couldn't know then was that Jim Land would retire in 1977 as a major, then go on to be elected secretary of the NRA, serving until 1999.

After everyone Muled back to the firing line, Captain Land took Chuck aside. "Whitby told me you're in a hurry to rejoin your outfit."

"That's right, sir. I'm helping Delta 1/5 and they're in for some serious stuff, sir."

"Throw your gear in my jeep. We'll give you a quick ride to your helicopter."

As they roared off toward the airport, Chuck didn't look back. It was like leaving the dentist's office—it hadn't been as bad as he thought, and it would be a long time before his next appointment.

# 30

# NATURE CAN KILL

Just before dawn, Chuck and his spotter, Carter, settled into a hide they'd chosen the day before, to the left of an abandoned hut and backed by tall trees. Come daylight, they'd be able to observe a vast open area where NVA activity had been reported.

As the day dawned, the men went to work. Chuck, on his belly, rested his long rifle on a bipod he'd crafted from bamboo, and began what might be hours of scoping the terrain. Carter leaned against a tree and searched with his binoculars. It was a beautiful morning, clean air, objects clear in the scope—a good day for hunting.

Suddenly there was rustling high up in the branches of a tree overhanging the hut. Fear shot up Chuck's spine as he swung his rifle toward the noise and frantically searched, but all he could see were huge magnified leaves. Pissed at his scope, he thought, *We should be dead now. How did we let the son of a bitch sneak up on us?* Carter shouldered his M14, ready for a shoot-out.

A giant green frog leapt out from high in the tree, landed on the hut's thatched roof, and jumped at full throttle, not looking back.

*Why is he in such a hurry?*

A snake fell coiling from a high branch and hit the roof. Chuck gaped at the five-footer—a viper, mouth wide open and gaining on the frog, who power-jumped off the roof out of sight, the snake in pursuit.

Chuck and Carter looked at each other with raised eyebrows and went back to work.

Hours later, Carter bumped Chuck's elbow; a silent signal, not urgent but an "I see something" bump. Chuck looked at Carter, who wore a crazy mouth-shut, not-laughing-out-loud grin. Carter pointed in the direction of one o'clock. Chuck turned his rifle until he picked out a pith helmet worn by a man wearing an NVA uniform squatting in some brush a few hundred yards away. The communist, feeling safely hidden, was relieving himself.

"Scope the bush to the man's right," said Carter.

"I see a reflection coming off something metallic," replied Chuck.

"It's a rifle barrel."

"For killing our marines."

Chuck waited for the man to stand up and fasten his pants. When the man picked up his AK-47, Chuck dispatched him.

# 31

# SMOKING GUN

During his monthly visits to An Hoa, marines continually invited Chuck to get high with them. "Don't knock it until you try it."

The Marine Corps didn't allow smoking weed out in the brush because it was of paramount importance to stay alert. However, in base camps, for many it was part of life.

Chuck was a drinker, not a pothead. He was leery. He'd heard you might never get over it. You might get paranoid. It could hippify you and you'd be against the war.

Then, an Alpha 1/5 marine dared him, "You ain't

got any balls if you don't power down some weed once
in a while."

"Okay, asshole," Chuck said. "There's nothing I
can't do better than you."

That night he followed the marine across the base to
where the tanks were lined up, looking like iron mon-
sters a dozen feet tall, barrels up like giant erections.
They stopped at one in the center. It was like the rest
except for a scattering of footprints in the dirt surrounding it. Chuck heard faint music reverberating through
the cast steel turret.

His buddy got serious then, scanning the area for
narcs, so it seemed. Seeing no one, he pulled out his Ka-
Bar and pounded out a code on the side of the tank, *dah
di-di dah dah . . . dah dah*! The music stopped. The turret
hatch flipped open, spewing sweet-smelling, red-tinged
smoke that gently hung in the cool Asian night.

*I can't believe I'm doing this,* Chuck thought, as he
followed his buddy, climbing up the cleats on the caterpillar tracks. Chuck looked down into the open hatch
through a red smoky haze—like hell itself.

"You first," invited his buddy.

Chuck entered feetfirst, slithering down into the bowels of the claustrophobic war machine. He stood there
on the tank's floorboards, eye to eye with a blinding, red-
painted light bulb. Squinting, he tried to get his where-
abouts. The bulb made everything look red, like the

lobby of a French whorehouse. Smoke burned Chuck's eyes.

He sank back, knee to knee with two men, sedentary hazy figures, their faces shadowy-red and scary with heavy eyelids. But their eyes were awake and suspicious.

The one with tank-commander goggles hanging from his neck and a roach clip clamped to the pocket of his tie-dyed dashiki harbored the stash between his legs, a plastic sandwich bag, half-full of the weed. He was also closest to the ashtray, made from a large shell casing and home to a smoldering joint. Chuck figured he was the chief stoner.

The man stared at Chuck.

Chuck stared back through watery eyes. He could stare down a wolf.

His buddy marine dropped into the space next to Chuck and gave the chief a nod. "Chuck's okay. He just wants to get turned on before he goes back out to the brush."

The chief clamped his roach clip to the end of the now-dead joint. Carefully gripping the clip in one hand and his Zippo in the other, he flicked the flame, lighting the joint like it was a sacred ritual. He pulled on his goggles and gazed at the flame of the fiery little weed as if expecting an idea might ooze into his skull.

Then he nodded the goggles to the man on his right—a guy with a Hawaiian shirt, a sling of beads, and a face flat as a shovel, who reached his arm up, exposing a skulled USMC tattoo, and turned up the transistor radio dangling from a remote machine gun trigger. The little radio squeaked out Joan Baez, singing "Saigon Bride."

*How appropriate,* Chuck thought. *Peace music in a manic killing machine. Am I the only one fighting this war?*

The chief took a toke from the joint, holding the smoke while passing it to the tattooed man, who sucked in a giant drag. He held the smoke in his lungs until he began to talk, his voice coming out as a high-pitched grunt as the vapor oozed from his nose and mouth.

The sound reminded Chuck of the noise coming from Grandpa's outhouse every morning.

The tattooed man's lungs emptied and his voice cracked, "Sing it, Joan."

Chuck still had doubts about becoming a pothead—*I don't fit in here*—just as the joint was passed to him. It was his turn.

On the other hand, he was not one to back out of a dare. *Booze never bothers me so why should this funny little cigarette?* He took a deep drag like it was one of his Marlboros. The smoke was hotter and heavier than he'd expected. No matter how much he tried not to, he began to cough and the more he coughed the more he needed to cough. The men laughed. Chuck coughed and they laughed. Chuck felt himself mellow.

Country Joe and the Fish came out of the little radio sounding like the New York Philharmonic. The red bulb hanging from the turret put out a beautiful crimson glow. The scary faces looked funny now. The men looked like clowns and jokers—their every movement exaggerated. Everything said was clever and comical. Chuck laughed. He liked these guys. He took another hit—a lighter one this time. But he coughed again and the men laughed.

A feeling of dread came over him. *They're laughing at me*. He felt ashamed of being a lightweight, so just to show them, he took another hit. The tank commander's goggles became twin kaleidoscopes staring at him. The skull tattoo grew teeth and laughed at him. Their quipster comments weren't funny anymore. He didn't like these guys anymore. He didn't want to be high anymore.

He nudged his buddy. "I wanna go."

His buddy laughed.

"No. I want out of here." Chuck rose from his seat.

The chief stared at Chuck as if judging him. "Bad trip, I guess. Better let him go."

Tattoo turned off the radio and the tank got quiet. Chuck wormed his way up through the turret in a hurry, sure he was locked in. He pushed the hatch open. It clanged like a bell when it bounced open on the turret, announcing to the whole world that there was a happening in the tank lot.

He stuck his head out. Everything was dark. Scary as hell. He searched the tank lot for narcs. They could be anywhere. *I'm being paranoid.*

He sucked in the unmolested oxygen and rolled out of the turret into the fresh air. Standing on the caterpillar cleats he heard the hatch click shut behind him. He leapt to the ground and chased away through the maze of tents and shadows and spine-chilling noises that followed him all the way to the snipers' tent.

Chuck tore open the flap and flopped on his cot.

He got worried again. *This is war,* he thought. *I'm in a war thousands of miles from home where the enemy is trying to kill me. They're trying to kill us all while everyone is sleeping and I'm the only one who gives a fuck.* He left the tent to check the guards on night duty.

Twice around the perimeter, the fresh air began to clear his head. He crawled onto his cot. He had a fitful time sleeping—falling in and out of nightmares, running and gunning, killing horrid-looking communists with fangs, as they came at him laughing, wielding daggers and AK-47s.

# 32

# WHITE-KNUCKLE RIDE

Late in Chuck's second tour, his squad leader, Mark Limpic, told him he was being sent alone with a Force Recon team for a four-day mission. US Marine Corps Force Reconnaissance is an elite group responsible for gathering information behind enemy lines. They'd be going straight west across the border into Laos. From his many missions, Chuck was familiar with the area but had never knowingly crossed the border.

"Meet them at the tarmac at 1700 this afternoon," said Mark, "and travel light."

On time at the tarmac, Chuck found the team of five, faces darkened, kerchiefs tied around their foreheads, fatigues with no emblems or names, carrying CAR-15 rifles—short-barreled wicked-looking automatic rifles—and lots of ammo. *A serious outfit,* Chuck thought. *Mark was right, they are traveling light.*

One introduced himself to Chuck as the team's 2nd Lieutenant (2 LT). While they waited for the helicopter, the 2 LT pulled out his map and explained the mission. He held the map up high so Chuck and the rest could see it. "This is where we're going," he said.

"It's upside down," Chuck said.

With a sheepish look, the 2 LT rotated the map so north was at the top. He continued, "Three LZs have been created for us by bombing holes in the three-canopy jungle near the border. They're about a thousand yards apart, here, here, and here," he said, pointing at the three LZs scribed on the map. "We'll drop into LZ-1 just before dark. Three days later we'll be picked up early morning at LZ-3."

*Whap-whap-whap.* A C-46 helicopter came flying out of the afternoon sun. An empty supply net hung from its underbelly. Reaching the LZ, the helicopter descended until the net was about a foot off the ground, rotating slowly in the blade wash.

Leaning into the wind, Chuck wondered, *Why are we standing out here with a supply helicopter? Where's our helicopter?*

"Jump on!" hollered the 2 LT.

The Force Recon team members climbed onto the net like a ride at an amusement park.

*Oh shit! This is what those poor-ass marines were training for back at Da Nang. The 2 LT must assume that I've trained for it.* It was too late for a discussion. Chuck grabbed the moving net and stepped on. As the helicopter rose, he clutched the net for dear life. Looking down, he saw the snipers' tent—his home. Outside it were his roomies, including Mark Limpic, pointing up at him, laughing at him.

After dangling from the helicopter for nearly thirty minutes that felt like hours, Chuck heard the machine throttle down. Soon he'd be on the ground—and, he hoped, unseen. The instant the net neared the ground, Chuck and the team hit the dirt, sprinted for the cover of the jungle, then followed the 2 LT on the run, struggling through the underbrush until it was too dark to continue. Chuck was impressed by their stealth—even at speed they were quiet.

As they prepared for the night, the team broke out in whispers. "Goddamn," one said, rubbing his back, "that safety strap nearly cut me in two."

"What safety strap?" Chuck asked.

"You weren't strapped on?" said the 2 LT.

Chuck shook his head and laughed. "Nope, no one told me about a strap. Or anything else, for that matter."

The Recon team laughed, while Chuck thought,

*I bet you wouldn't be laughing if I'd fallen off and splattered.*

The 2 LT pulled out his map again. Chuck looked at it over the 2 LT's shoulder. A circle was drawn just inside Laos. The 2 LT explained the rest of the mission. They were to find and observe a large group of NVA who'd been spotted in a village inside the circle.

At first light, Chuck and the team left where they'd spent the night and moved through the jungle searching most of the day. Again Chuck appreciated how they moved catlike through the underbrush. So different from traveling with grunts who tromped like a high school band down Main Street on the 4th of July.

Toward evening they found the village and settled into a good hide about six hundred yards out, from where they could safely observe NVA inside the village.

By day three, it was obvious to Chuck which NVA was in charge—an officer who often came out of a hut and strutted around like a rooster, calling out orders. Assuming the officer was the target, Chuck found an elevated place in the brush close to the team, where, lying prone, he could see the front of the leader's hut. It would be easy: wait until he came out then plug him. All he had to do now was wait until the 2 LT gave him the green light.

Later in the day, the 2 LT told Chuck and the team to get ready to leave.

"So, when do I shoot the guy?" asked Chuck.

"You're not to shoot the guy or anyone else."

Chuck was confused. If he wasn't going to shoot anyone, why had he been sent?

The 2 LT announced to the team, "We're going to LZ-2 for extraction."

"You told us we'd be picked up at LZ-3," Chuck said. "You showed us on the map."

The 2 LT twisted his face, looking undecided.

"With all due respect, sir," said Chuck, "I'm going to LZ-3."

The other men concurred, nodding at the 2 LT.

The 2 LT sighed. "Okay, let's go."

The team started off single file, the 2 LT in the lead. They came to a small valley. Out came the map again, and the 2 LT said, "We'll go across through the middle of this valley and we'll find LZ-3 just on the other side."

"Sir," said Chuck, "may I see your map?"

Rolling his eyes, the 2 LT handed it to him.

"LZ-3 isn't where you say it is." Chuck pointed at the map. "It's over the next rise here. And if we go through the middle of the valley we'll probably get our asses shot. It would be better to traverse the hillside, which has more cover."

"Okay," the 2 LT said. "You seem to know your way around. Let's go."

The next morning, Chuck and the team awoke in brush close to LZ-3. They stayed hidden, waiting for the CH-46 to arrive. Hearing the helicopter, Chuck gritted his teeth thinking of the net ride back, but at least this time he'd be strapped on for safety.

The helicopter appeared—no net. Chuck was elated. It landed and dropped its tailgate. Chuck and the team ran for it, jumped in, and made a clean getaway.

Back at An Hoa, Chuck told Mark, "Don't send me on a mission like that one again. That 2 LT doesn't know a map from his ass."

Mark smiled. "That's why you were sent."

## 33

# CHANGE OF OCCUPATION

**C**huck had only two weeks left of his second tour. Marine Corps regulations wouldn't allow him another tour as a scout sniper, so he accepted that in two weeks, he'd be leaving Vietnam for good. Then after furlough, he would serve out his remaining time stateside doing what, he didn't know.

First, he was called into An Hoa to wait out his tour. His spotter, Joseph Ward, followed him to the waiting helicopter to say goodbye.

Leaning into the blade wash, Chuck reluctantly handed over his rifle to Ward. Over the noise, Chuck hollered, "Take good care of my baby!" He turned and stepped into the helicopter.

At An Hoa, Chuck volunteered to spend his remaining two weeks on night-guard duty. With an M14 equipped with a starlight scope, he marked up two more kills.

He knew his total number of confirmed kills was 103. What he didn't know was that he'd just become the US Marine Corps' deadliest sniper.

During those two weeks, Chuck realized he wasn't ready to leave Vietnam. So he re-upped for a third tour, putting in for helicopter door gunner with MAG 11 (1st Marine Division Air Group) located in Da Nang.

His trip home was much like the other but he knew from before what to expect and what to ignore. He spent the time home with family and returned to Vietnam by the same route as before.

Back in Da Nang, Chuck reported to the MAG 11 compound to be interviewed for his new job as helicopter door gunner. But the officer, a chaplain, was concerned about Chuck becoming a gunner because of his prior job as sniper. He was afraid Chuck would be gun-happy and possibly shoot innocent civilians on the ground, so he denied Chuck the position. Chuck wasn't happy being turned down, especially for something he knew wouldn't happen.

Chuck reported to the CO at MAG 11, who made

him head of security for the compound—"top cop"—with a police force in charge of the compound, the airport, and even the little brig to lock up soldiers who got too drunk and rowdy. Chuck didn't care much for the job and the responsibility that came with it. He wasn't hard on the revelers. He knew the need to blow off steam. He could usually talk them into going home, saving them from the brig.

Though his new job pretty much sucked, there were some perks that came with it. Often he accompanied officers to provide security on trips inside Vietnam and junkets to other countries.

Once he was sent with a captain on a flight to Thailand. The captain had business on the base and, with Chuck in tow, went about the day doing what officers do.

At the end of the day, the captain said, "We're done here."

"You ready to fly back to Da Nang, sir?" Chuck asked.

"No. All this stressful shit has made me thirsty. How about a drink at the officers' club?"

"Good idea, sir," said Chuck. "But you know I can't go in there. I'm an enlisted man."

"No problem," said the captain, reaching in his briefcase. He pulled out an extra pair of captain bars, pinned them on Chuck's collar, smoothed out Chuck's shirt, and said, "Let's go."

Entering the club—*uh-oh*—a familiar-looking

captain was sitting at a table. Chuck had worked for the man during his first tour.

"Hello, *Captain* Mawhinney," the officer said.

Chuck knew he'd been caught. Impersonating an officer was a serious offense that offered time in the brig. "It's been awhile, sir," he said, and followed his charge to the bar.

The man must have liked Chuck because he didn't blow the whistle on him.

# 34

# GOODBYE VIETNAM

After completing the six months of his third and final tour, Chuck said his last goodbye to Vietnam. He was sent back to Camp Pendleton, San Diego, where he was given the job of drill instructor. He was okay with rousing the recruits every morning at oh-dark-thirty and putting them through a hard day of physical endurance. But having to yell at them at the same time wasn't Chuck's cup of tea.

One day in the mess hall Chuck bumped into a company commander he had worked for in Vietnam.

"Mawhinney, what in the world are you doing here?" the officer asked.

"I'm a drill instructor, sir," said Chuck.

"What? Why aren't you down at the range teaching your shooting skills?"

Chuck shrugged. "You don't ask the Corps why, sir."

"I'll be looking into this," the officer said.

Soon Chuck was reassigned as a preliminary marksman instructor (PMI) on the rifle range at Camp Pendleton. Because of his rank of sergeant and his expertise, he was put in charge of the other instructors at the range. Chuck was happy returning to what he loved most: shooting.

One day, he was sent to teach naval officer candidates the nomenclature of the M16 rifle. At times, during class, Chuck asked for questions. When a candidate raised his hand, Chuck pointed to him and said, "Okay, asshole," a common way to address a fellow marine.

During the class, some naval brass entered the room and took seats and began observing. Chuck continued using "asshole" to recognize a candidate with a question.

During a break, one of the officers approached Chuck saying, "Mawhinney, you are doing an outstanding job with the class."

"Thank you, sir."

"Just one thing." The officer lowered his voice. "Some of these men will become officers in the United States Navy and they like being called candidates, not assholes."

"Yessir," Chuck replied, thinking, *I'd better watch my mouth*.

The officer sat down to resume observing.

At the end of the next segment, Chuck asked for questions again. A candidate raised his hand. Chuck pointed at the young man and said without thinking, "Okay, asshole." *Oops*. He threw the officer a quick glance.

The officer shook his head and, with his cohorts, walked out of the room.

The ways of the Corps are not easily changed and Chuck continued to refer to the candidates as "assholes."

With troop downsizing in Vietnam, the Marine Corps announced soldiers could get out early, providing they didn't owe the Corps any money or other obligations.

So on August 1, 1970, then Sergeant Chuck Mawhinney packed his duffel bag for home. In it were his discharge papers (DD 214), a Bronze Star medal with Combat-V, Navy Achievement Medal, Navy Commendation Medal with Combat-V, The Republic of Vietnam Gallantry Cross with Palm, and two Purple Hearts.

He rumbled out of the base in his hot rod GTO Pontiac, saying goodbye to the US Marine Corps. Looking ahead and not behind, he drove almost nonstop to Lakeview.

Right away he went looking for work. He loved the outdoors, driving machinery, and the smell of diesel, so he went to the nearest US Forest Ranger station where they worked outside with big equipment, and pleaded his case. He returned day after day until he was hired as a temp in the engineering department, drafting and working with the survey crew. Desiring a permanent job, Chuck took the civil engineering test, passing it with eighty-five points, plus ten points for being a Purple Heart veteran, totaling 95. He was hired, and that's how his US Forest Service career began.

Later that year, Chuck moved to the road crew that was responsible for maintaining roads in the forest for recreation and logging operations. Chuck loved to run the dozers and other heavy equipment. The Forest Service considered it a blue-collar job, but it paid better than General Schedule positions.

Chuck also hired out to Lake County in the winter, running a snowplow at night. Chuck was real busy and liked it that way.

But then . . .

# 35

# CHUCK FINDS A CURE FOR PTSD

**C**huck began having nightmares, like the man who got away, still staring at him through those god-awful dark eyes.

Chuck had been raised to follow the Ten Commandments, such as "Thou shalt not kill." Then as a teenage marine he'd been licensed to kill. After seeing his buddies brutally killed, he'd grown a thirst for vengeance. He'd spent two tours—nineteen months—killing other human beings. He'd had the enemy in his sights hundreds of times, having to decide if the man would live or die, an extreme rush—the ultimate hunt and kill, and the ultimate payback: revenge. Counting unconfirmed kills, Chuck had averaged four kills a week, more than most companies.

Meanwhile, he had heard what the enemy did to American snipers if they caught one. Because of Chuck's reputation, the enemy would have known of him and how many of their fellow countrymen had died with a Mawhinney bullet torn in their skull. Among those Vietnamese kids filling sandbags for the marines at An Hoa, some could have been Viet Cong sympathizers and outed him. Chuck would have been a big prize.

In combat, he'd never known from day to day or night to night which bullet or land mine would kill or maim him.

He'd figured he'd never make it home alive.

Now, back in Lakeview, there was no one who could understand what he'd been through. No one could have the faintest idea what he felt like. So, he kept it to himself. He told no one, not even his family. No one.

Seeking a change and more opportunity for advancement with the Forest Service, Chuck transferred to the Olympic National Forest in the state of Washington, for a job in road maintenance near the small town of Quilcene. With his sleeping bag, one suitcase full of clothes, and half a case of beer, Chuck made a quick trip in his Datsun 240Z.

After checking in at the office, Chuck went looking for a place to stay and stepped into the first beer joint he saw, the Whistling Oyster. There he met a man named Joe who rented him a room. Chuck and Joe became friends over like interests—beer drinking, fast cars, and hot chicks.

Chuck began working in the forest, driving and maintaining heavy machinery: Cats, graders, and backhoes. He was well-liked and respected. On time for work every morning and good at his job.

Nighttime was different. At five o'clock, after working like Dr. Jekyll all day, Chuck piled into his car. Backing out, checking the rearview mirror, Mr. Hyde grinned back at him. He rushed to the Whistling Oyster for the beers and the friends. There were girls there, too, and it was the 1970s—free love. Chuck flirted with the girls and sometimes got lucky. If not, he closed the place.

On weekday mornings he was up early for work, often with a pounding headache, hustling to his car through pouring rain that reminded him of Vietnam monsoons, but colder. Quilcene sogged under two hundred inches a year. Backing his car into the storm, he checked his rearview mirror to see not a happy Mr. Hyde but a stern Dr. Jekyll glaring back at him.

Sometimes in the mornings Chuck swore to himself he wouldn't go back to the Whistling Oyster, but then by five o'clock, Mr. Hyde was speeding for the tavern.

One day, Chuck got a call from Dennis, who was still in the Army and stationed in Fort Lewis, Washington. Dennis was about to be discharged and move back to Oregon. He was married with a growing family and too many cars. He couldn't keep his almost-finished V-8 hot rod model A roadster. Chuck thought about it—he didn't need the added expense and didn't have a garage for it—but he knew that the girls around Quilcene liked guys with hot-looking fast-assed cars. He could see himself driving around town with a hot rod full of girls.

"I'll help you out of that little problem, Dennis. Bring it over and we'll work out the details." So, after the first winter was over and the days warmed and the rain slowed, Dennis brought the hot rod to Chuck's house.

When summer came, Chuck and Joe worked weekends finishing up and maintaining the hot rod. Chuck kept the motor tuned in case some guy got roostered up and wanted to race. He drove both his cars like a wild man with a beer clamped between his knees, Mr. Hyde white-faced hanging on, outracing Dr. Jekyll.

For instance, during one Friday-night race, Chuck burned up the clutch in his hot rod. The closest parts house with a new clutch was in Port Angeles, forty-seven miles away, and required the old clutch as a trade-in. Removing a clutch is a time-consuming job. So, Chuck and

Joe started early Saturday and by late afternoon they had the clutch on the ground.

Chuck checked his watch—forty-five minutes to closing.

Old clutch along, the boys jumped in the Z car. Chuck slammed the throttle and attacked the winding road, passing cars on blind corners and cutting it close—cheating death by inches. He made the suicide trip in thirty-five minutes.

Joe, who was also reckless and courageous at times, might have enjoyed the ride or was in fear of dying with a crazy man who seemed intent on killing himself.

Chuck and Joe made other hell-bent trips to Seattle for the thrill of the big city. Seattle was a Navy town. The bars were full of a younger crowd with Navy ships coming and going in the harbor. When the huge gunships left port, Chuck and Joe were handy to rescue the teary-eyed girlfriends and wives by helping them drown their sorrows with drinks offered by the understanding Romeos.

After three years of the fast life and the god-awful rain, Chuck longed for Oregon, where life was slower and the sun could shine. He transferred to the Siuslaw National Forest, west of Eugene, and moved into a rented cabin six miles up the Siuslaw River from the secluded little town of Mapleton, Oregon. There was a tavern with a local clientele of young people, and it was still the 1970s—mountain hippie chicks and free love. And of course, Mr. Hyde rode along.

Chuck's job at Mapleton was assistant to road maintenance foreman. He drove and repaired heavy machines, fixing gravel roads in and around the forest. Soon the foreman moved on and Chuck got the job as boss over the dozen men on the crew.

There was a young office employee named Robin Hood (yeah, that's what Chuck thought). She lived with her parents two miles downstream from Chuck on the opposite side of the river. He was attracted to her but she was too young—in fact, she couldn't legally drink yet. Chuck left her alone for a while, letting her grow up some.

But one dark rainy night, in his cabin alone, he began to think about Robin. So he called and asked her to come spend the night at his house. She was game.

Excited and into the beer a ways, he said he'd come for her if she'd return with him the same way. And again she was game.

Chuck drove in the dark the two miles downstream and parked beside the river, Robin's porch light twinkling in the rain across the water. He tore off his shirt and shoes and dove in. *Oh fuck!* The water was like ice. He swam as hard as he could trying to pull across the current and realized he'd made a mistake. He was tiring; the cold river was swallowing him. He might die.

Well, wasn't that what he wanted? Hadn't he been trying to kill himself all this time?

No, he hadn't wanted to die. It was more like he wasn't scared to. Now he would drown in a harmless little river.

He reached shore—he wouldn't die that night. He climbed the slippery bank through blackberry bushes that clawed him with their razor-sharp thorns. He limped out onto a gravel road.

Robin's mom answered the door. She was sure this stranger had wrecked his car in the river so invited him in. Chuck entered, dripping and bleeding on the rug. He explained he'd swum the river to see Robin.

"Robin!" Mom yelled up the stairs for her daughter. "There's someone here to see you!"

Robin came out of her room at the top of the stairs with her overnight case. She looked at Chuck, rolled her eyes, and went back into her room.

Mom gave Chuck a towel to dry off. Robin bounced down the stairs with her overnight case inside a garbage bag. She was going to swim back with him.

Chuck was impressed. Mom was worried. But she waved goodbye as Chuck followed Robin up the river. They walked in the dark about a hundred yards to where a fishing cabin hung off the bank. If they would swim from here, she told him, they'd come out where he'd parked his car.

They plunged in, swimming hard and laughing through the frigid water. They stepped out of the river right where she said they would.

Chuck had met his match. Robin was a keeper.

# 36

# TRAPPING WITH A MOUNTAIN MAN

They were married in Mapleton. Later in Mapleton, two boys joined the family.

In 1981, Chuck transferred to the Wallowa-Whitman National Forest, based in Baker City, Oregon, surrounded by Swiss Alps–looking mountains. He soon found the local tavern, the Idle Hour, and at the same time he kept up his family obligations—another boy joined the household.

Chuck liked the Idle Hour, a little mill-rat tavern. Sometime in 1985, he met George Gill there. George was known as an ornery old bastard. Chuck guessed he was about fifty-five. He reminded him of a gnarly old mountain man of yesteryear. Chuck was taken by his gravelly voice and steely blue eyes.

Over beers, George told Chuck he was a government trapper.

Chuck was intrigued with trapping. He knew that successful trappers had to find where the animals worked and coax them into a trap—much like what he'd done in Vietnam. He wanted to try trapping, so he dogged old George with questions. He must have asked the right questions because George warmed up to him and told him about his trapping. How he controlled the bobcat and coyote populations in Baker County. Bobcats kill domestic animals as large as lambs. Coyotes run in packs, killing lambs, goats, and calves.

"I've even seen 'em chewing on an old mother cow," said George.

"Wow, cows are big," said Chuck. "Can't they defend themselves?"

"Not while down and giving birth," replied George.

One day at the Idle Hour George invited Chuck to go trapping. The next Friday they met at George's house at dawn, piled into George's old Ford filled with smelly traps and furs, and hit the road for the hills. Gruff old George told Chuck that when they got to trapping he should keep his questions to himself and pay attention and learn. The Friday trapping session became a weekly event. As they got to know each other better, they began swapping hunting stories and found they had a lot in common.

One Friday, while trapping with George, Chuck saw coyotes running in open country, which gave him an idea. "Hey, George, I could shoot a few of those dogs and save us some trapping."

"You really think you can hit them little bastards on the run?"

The next Friday, Chuck brought his .22-250. At first light, George and Chuck left the pickup and right away Chuck spotted a coyote a couple hundred yards out, on a dead-ass run across a pasture. Chuck pulled up on him and fired, tipping the coyote end over end.

George pulled off his wool cap, scratched his head, and said, "Sum' bitch."

Spring came, and the mother coyotes were kegged-up in dens with their young, making trapping difficult. So during the week, George located dens, then Fridays he led Chuck within eyesight and earshot of a den and they hid close by. George blew on his whistle— a bone-chilling cry of a rabbit in pain—inviting the mother to come out for dinner. Chuck shot the coyote. Sometimes other coyotes made the mistake of showing up to share the "rabbit" and Chuck and George made multiple kills at one den. Then George gassed the den, and the pups entered eternal sleep. Because coyote pelts are in bad shape in spring, the hunters left the carcasses for the vultures and moved on to another den.

In the fall, when all the coyotes were out and about, George used his traps again. He checked them daily. The pelts were in good shape, so he skinned them on the spot. On Fridays, Chuck helped. George made skinning look easy. But Chuck's first took twenty minutes. Soon, using George's tricks, the chore shortened to three minutes. Back at George's, Chuck helped stretch the pelts over frames and hang them outside on the garage wall to dry.

In 1997, at the age of forty-eight, having worked for the federal government for thirty years, including his time in the USMC, Chuck retired. With time on his hands, he decided to run his own trapline. He got a trapping license, bought some used traps, and went to the mountains overlooking Durkee, Oregon, to see if he could catch a bobcat.

After a few weeks with no bobcat, he asked George to go with him to see what he was doing wrong. Arriving in the canyon where Chuck had been trapping, George asked where Chuck had set his trap. Chuck pointed up at about a dozen places around the canyon. George laughed and told Chuck he only needed one trap for the whole area, to wait for the soon expected snow, then follow the cat's tracks to see where it went and what its habits were.

After the next snowfall, he followed the cat's tracks over the side of the mountain, noting its habits and hiding spots. He set a single trap and two days later caught the bobcat.

Chuck began taking his trio of boys along on his trapping and hunting adventures. He taught them to use their senses like he'd learned from Fofo. He taught them to study the habits of the game they were hunting—"Think like they think."

Then the fur prices fell and coincidentally gas prices rose. It didn't pay to continue trapping. Chuck and Robin quit the business. But the family continued to hunt and fish.

George became like a father to Chuck. They would remain hunting partners until George's death in June 2007 at the age of seventy-six.

# 37

# OUTED BY JOE

**B**ack in 1993, Chuck got a phone call from Joseph Ward, his last spotter in Vietnam. Ward told him he'd published a book called *Dear Mom: A Sniper's Vietnam*, and he'd included their time together.

Chuck was surprised and dismayed. He'd kept this part of his life hidden and now was wary of the outcome of being outed.

Sounding distraught then, Ward told Chuck that the authors of *Death from Afar*, a series of books about marine scout snipers, had disputed Ward's claim that Chuck had 101 confirmed kills. World-renowned marine scout sniper Carlos Hathcock held the record of most kills at

93. The dispute had stirred controversy in the military and shooting communities, who asked, "Who is this Chuck Mawhinney who claims to have more kills than Carlos Hathcock?"

Ward asked Chuck if the number 101 was correct.

Chuck told Ward it was wrong—the number was 103. Chuck explained that after he'd given Ward his rifle and went back to An Hoa, he'd confirmed two more kills.

Soon after, Chuck got a phone call from Norm Chandler, one of the coauthors of the sniper series. Chandler said Joe Ward's claim of 101 was untrue.

Chuck agreed. Chandler was astonished.

Chuck told him that the correct number was 103. Chandler expressed his doubt.

Chuck wasn't used to having his honesty questioned. It left a sour taste in his mouth. Coolly, he suggested Chandler contact Mark Limpic, his wartime squad leader, who would confirm his record.

Three years later in 1996, Chuck got a phone call from Peter Senich, author of several books about snipers. While researching for his next book, *The One-Round War*, Senich had come across a newspaper article that mentioned Chuck and the controversy of his number of kills. Chuck reassured him. Senich believed him but had to confirm it for his book. Through Senich's connections with the USMC archives, he saw Chuck's kill sheets confirming 103.

Senich revealed his findings in a Q and A article in *Precision Shooting* magazine. Also in the article, he mentioned that Chuck's sniper rifle had been found, taken out of service, and sent to Eric Reed, a marine armorer. Reed had restored the rifle, and now it was on display at the USMC museum in Quantico.

Later in 1996, the Chandler brothers published their fifth book in the series, acknowledging Chuck's record of 103, surpassing Carlos Hathcock's record of 93.

Chuck was officially the Marine Corps' deadliest sniper.

Later yet in 1996, Chuck got his first invitation to speak publicly. The event was the graduation ceremony of the Marine Scout Sniper School in Quantico, Virginia. A nervous Chuck spoke in front of hundreds of graduates and their families. After the ceremony, he met the Chandler brothers. Animosity between the men blew away in the Virginia wind.

In the spring of 1997, Chuck got another invitation to speak, this time as guest of honor for the NRA international sniper shooting competition at the Whittington Center in Raton, New Mexico. Becoming comfortable in front of a crowd, Chuck gave his talk on long-distance shooting and presented the awards to the best shooters from several countries including Germany, Austria, and Czechoslovakia.

In the fall of 1997, Chuck was startled by a request

to do his first interview in front of a TV camera, for a documentary called *The Science of Guns*. Chuck was leery of the camera, but the documentary was a success mostly due to Chuck's ability to tell a story.

In January of 1998, newspaper writer Jayson Jacoby called Chuck. He wanted to write a story in the local *Baker City Herald* about Chuck's sniper career. Chuck agreed, answering his questions in his usual calm, quiet, humorous manner. Jacoby's article covered Chuck's life from marine sniper up until his recent retirement.

The AP wire service picked up the story and spread it around to several papers throughout the United States. Chuck immediately received phone calls from all over the country thanking him for what he had done in war.

The first Friday after the article came out, Chuck stepped into the Idle Hour to meet up with friends as usual. But they stared at him, speechless. They wouldn't talk to him or go near him. Surprised and confused, Chuck wondered, *Why are they acting this way? Oh— they must have read Jacoby's article. Now they know. Maybe they don't know what to say. Or maybe they feel guilty for not going to war? Or is it because I hid my past from them? Or are they scared of me?*

For the first time in his life, Chuck drank beer alone.

Meanwhile at home, Chuck's mailbox began filling with letters—some good and some not so good. For instance, a couple sent a letter saying their son was a trained sniper who had been sent to prison for killing a man. They wondered if Chuck would write a letter to the parole board saying it was the military's fault and to please release him. Chuck was touched by their concern for their son. But he didn't know the circumstances of the killing so he couldn't do anything for them. Saying no to the family was hard for Chuck. Thankfully, the disturbing letters tapered off and the good ones kept coming.

Back at the Idle Hour the coldness went on for over a month. He considered moving away. But before he could arrange it, his friends began to return, some sheepishly, but they were back and no one talked about Vietnam much and Chuck was happy again.

# 38

# ACCEPTING CELEBRITY

**L**ate in 1999, Chuck received a phone call from Tony Perry, a writer for the *Los Angeles Times*, requesting an interview. Chuck wondered why a giant newspaper like the *Times* wanted to know about him. But they must have wanted it bad, because Perry traveled all the way to Chuck's kitchen table to get the interview.

Over coffee, Perry began asking questions. Chuck sensed the writer was after a horrible war story. Chuck, who looks on the brighter side of things and can make fun of any situation, told Perry that there was a lot more to being a sniper than shooting people. Like being the eyes and ears for company missions and, when back at the base, cleaning his rifle and burning shitters.

Perry's article, "A Sniper at Peace with His Duties," came out March 10, 2000. Right away it picked up national and international attention. Again the phone calls and letters came rolling in. As before, some were good, and some were not so good. Chuck changed his phone number. Then, when things cooled again, he changed it back.

In January 2000, CNN asked Chuck to be part of a documentary they were doing about the twenty-fifth anniversary of the United States pulling out of Vietnam. Chuck suggested filming the interview at a shooting competition in Phoenix, where he was to talk about sniping in Vietnam.

They consented. At the hotel in Phoenix, the interview started with questions about snipers. Chuck soon got the drift that the interviewer wanted to present snipers as bad boys of war. He stopped the interviewer and invited him and the film crew to sit in on his presentation.

In the hotel conference room, with the CNN crew listening in the back, Chuck told the crowd a similar rendition of what he'd told Perry of the *Los Angeles Times,* including the part about burning shitters.

When Chuck's presentation concluded and the crowd had left, the interviewer resumed with questions that had softened. To Chuck's delight, it turned out that his knowledge of the subject and quiet manner had won the interviewer over. It was a great day for marine scout snipers.

Later in 2000, Chuck was invited to speak at his first symposium, held in Baltimore, Maryland, sponsored by Operational Tactics Inc. It was his biggest audience yet. While speaking to the five hundred attendees, he showed slides of his personal experiences in the Vietnam War. He explained how snipers were experts on map reading because they had to know exactly where they were at all times, day and night. He described how snipers snooped on the enemy to predict their future movements. He told how they shot an occasional VC who was lying in wait to kill marines.

At a gun show in the winter of 2000, Chuck happened upon a booth with a large sign bearing the name Strider Knives, a new company that made military-style knives. He stopped to take a peek. The booth was manned by a small group of young marines showing knives to potential customers while drinking beer.

Seeing the suds flowing, Chuck was naturally drawn in. Introductions were made and a conversation followed. During war stories told back and forth over beers, the marines learned that Chuck had been a marine in Vietnam. He drained his beer and moved on to see more of the gun show.

Coincidentally or with a thirst, Chuck happened by the booth again. The marines welcomed him back with new looks of respect. Chuck wondered what that was about. Then one confessed he'd snooped on his computer and discovered Chuck was a famous sniper. Chuck wasn't surprised—his name was all over computers by then.

Many beers and stories later, a marine blurted, "Hey, let's get Strider to make a Chuck Mawhinney knife. It'll be just like the Ka-Bar he carried in Vietnam with Chuck Mawhinney etched on it and it'll sell millions. And of course Chuck will get royalties off 'em."

Chuck was amazed they thought his name would make the knife sell.

Strider did build the knife and many were sold. Chuck is proud that Strider Knives awarded a Chuck Mawhinney knife to the top shooter at all USMC sniper graduations.

⊕

While being flown all over the country for interviews and speaking engagements, Chuck began to be recognized in a crowd, which always surprised him. For example, in a bar on the concourse at the airport in Minneapolis/St. Paul, a man stared at Chuck as if searching his memory, then exclaimed, "I saw you on TV! You're Chuck Mawhinney!" He bought Chuck a few beers.

Chuck didn't know whether to like all the attention or not. He is still amazed by it.

Chuck appreciated all the benefits that had come from being a scout sniper and looked for opportunities to pass on his skills. In 2003, Chuck met two experts in police strategy and got an idea. They teamed up, using their combined skills to teach police "high-risk entry," "man tracking," and other useful tactics.

# 39

# REUNIONS

In June 2003 Chuck was in Atlanta in the Strider Knife booth, helping promote the knife they'd designed honoring Chuck (it would be featured on the cover of the August 2003 *Blade* magazine).

While Chuck was busy with some knife enthusiasts, he noticed some young marines waiting to speak with him.

"Are you Chuck Mawhinney?" the dark-haired one asked.

Chuck smiled. "That depends."

The tallest one asked Chuck what it was like fighting in Vietnam.

"It was humid, we burned shitters, there were big snakes, and the C-Rations sucked."

"Is that all you got to eat was C-Rats?" asked the dark-haired one.

"That's all we ate when in the field, except one time we barbequed a pig."

"How's that?" asked the one in the back.

Chuck told them about how this helicopter pilot had flown a wandering pig he'd shot back to camp. And how Fofo had roasted the thing in the ground and how good it was.

"I know that pilot," said the dark-haired one. "I've heard him tell the exact same story."

"No way," Chuck said. "You know how many helicopter pilots were in Vietnam?"

"I'll prove it," the marine said. "He's here at the show. Stay put and I'll get him."

Chuck kept visiting with the remaining marines until the dark-haired marine returned with a man about Chuck's age, who said, "You the guy who shot the pig?"

"Well, I shot *a* pig," Chuck said, still doubtful.

"Was it at Liberty Bridge in '69?"

Curious then, Chuck said, "Sure was. There were two of us; my spotter Bill and myself."

The pilot's face brightened. "My crew chief was having a cow about loading the bloody pig in the bird— thought it was too messy."

Chuck stood and shook the man's hand. "My name's Chuck. Thanks for getting us out that day."

After the show closed for the night, Chuck and the pilot reunited at the hotel bar, hammering down beers and reminiscing about Vietnam.

Since 2010, Robin, with occasional help from Mark Limpic, has arranged four sniper reunions.

The first one was Robin's surprise to Chuck. Chuck was happy. She and Mark had invited eight snipers from the platoon and their families to meet up in Las Vegas at the Monte Carlo casino.

First thing at the 2010 reunion, the snipers gathered in the casino conference room over beers and snacks. It had been years since Chuck and the others had seen each other. Chuck found himself asking over and over, "You still alive?" A lot of beer was guzzled and many stories were told within the group of aging daredevils.

Nine years later, while planning an all-guy snipers-only reunion, Robin learned the platoon had lost a brother, but she found a few more. The still rowdy marines needed a different venue where they could get drunk and hoot and holler some, so Robin rented them two adjoining houses in Las Vegas. Ten snipers showed up.

When Robin was organizing an all-family reunion for 2012, a sniper's son suggested they move the reunion to Pensacola, Florida, where he was connected, so she did. She found the platoon had lost another brother, but again she located a new one. Snipers and their families stayed in condos not far from the Pensacola air base where Marine Corps pilots train. First thing, the snipers flocked to the pool area, where they happened to meet young marine aviators from the base who reveled in the old snipers' stories of the Vietnam War.

The same sniper's son organized a motorcade for the snipers and families to sightsee the Pensacola area. On returning to the condo, the motorcade was met by a large gang of bikers who were lined up on both sides of the street. Chuck wondered what the hell was going on. The motorcade slowed—the bikers raised American flags like sabers and saluted as the old warriors motored through.

Sharing beer with the bikers around the pool, Chuck asked a gray-bearded one, "What's this all about?"

"We're the Patriot Guard. One of your kids invited us. Normally we honor bodies of deceased veterans. It's nice to honor the living for a change."

"It's better to be seen than viewed." Chuck grinned.

# 40

# REPLICATING CHUCK'S REMINGTON

**B**ack in 2000, after speaking at the Baltimore symposium, Chuck was introduced to Andrew Evans-Hendrick of the UK. Hendrick owned Riflecraft Ltd, a business that specialized in training professional shooters as well as building and modifying military rifles. Hendrick was impressed by Chuck's enthusiasm for his Remington 700 sniper rifle. He was equally enthused about Chuck's gun. Hendrik suggested they team up to create replicas.

Chuck agreed, and excitement built between the two men as they discussed and planned the project. Their goal was to build 103 commemorative rifles exactly like the one Chuck shot so successfully in Vietnam. They would personalize each rifle by engraving each one with Chuck's signature and an individual number, 001 through 103—one for each of Chuck's confirmed kills.

Armed with Hendrick's contacts and expertise and Chuck's legendary name and authorization, the two men approached Remington Arms Company about building the basic rifle. Remington agreed to the project.

The military projects manager for Remington Arms, Michael Haugen, a Special Forces sniper himself, built the 103 rifles in Remington's custom shop.

Next, Chuck and Hendrick hired George Gardner of G.A. Precision to free-float the heavy twenty-four-inch barrels and pillar-bed the actions. Gardner also oversaw the engraving of the bolt side of each receiver with Chuck's initials, CBM, and the number 8541, the USMC designation for scout sniper. He had the floor plates of each rifle engraved with Chuck's signature along with numbers 001–103.

To produce a correct Redfield 3–9X scope, Chuck and Hendrick went to Leupold, the optics company that at the time owned Redfield rifle scopes. Leupold agreed to re-create the scopes and turned the project over to their vice president of military branches, Kevin Trepa, a former marine officer, who oversaw the building of the scopes.

Next up, they needed mounts to attach the scopes to the rifles. Chuck and Hendrick discovered that Badger Ordnance, a business specializing in scope mounts, happened to have an original M40 mount just like Chuck's that had been modified to fit the Redfield scopes. Badger made 103 exact reproductions of the mounts for the rifles.

In 2012, the finished engraved rifles, weighing 9¾ pounds—the exact weight as Chuck's original—were sent to him. In his garage, he attached the scopes to the rifles. Then at the local gun range, using 175 grain Black Hills match ammo, Chuck broke in each individual rifle and filled out and signed its logbook and target, then packed it with that rifle in a black Plano case.

Chuck is pleased that all 103 rifles have been sold.

# AUTHOR LOOKING BACK

As I write this, it's been four years since my first visit with Chuck in his garage. He gave me his blessing to write this book. I was humbled by his trust in me.

But with the opportunity to write his life story came the responsibility for the outcome.

Would the book live up to Chuck's life?

I knew I would give it my all: the research, the travel, the hours and hours in front of a computer screen. And this was the easy part. The hard part would be interviewing Chuck. I knew he'd kept his life in war hidden for years. I'd be digging up what he'd buried. Then sifting through the horror of it all.

I worried how he'd deal with the memories.

After our second meeting in his garage, my concerns vanished.

Then Robin called me. Chuck was having nightmares. She was worried it was because of the book.

I didn't want him to suffer—his well-being mattered more than anything.

I told Robin I was dropping the project. I assured her I was okay with it.

She seemed relieved.

A few months later, Chuck called me and said, "I want you to write the book."

"You sure? What about the nightmares?"

He laughed. "What's a few bad dreams?"

# ACKNOWLEDGMENTS

Thank you, editorial consultant C. Lill Ahrens, for sharing your knowledge and relentless enthusiasm with me for this project.